THE MANCHESTER TROLLEYBUS

Michael Eyre and Chris Heaps

With chapters by
Philip Groves and Fred Eversfield
and additional material by
Peter Thompson, Keith Walker, Howard Piltz and Geoff Burrows

Featuring photography by
Ray Dunning, Peter Thompson, Howard Piltz,
Tony Belton, Chris Bennett, Peter Caunt, Ted Jones,
Don Jones, John Kaye and Reg Wilson

Ian Allan
PUBLISHING

Contents

COVER front
Bound for Stalybridge on the 218, BUT 1329 passes London Road Fire Station. Dating from 1906, the headquarters of the Manchester City Fire Brigade was acknowledged as the finest in the country. The baroque buff, terracotta and red brick building had a central courtyard with balconies giving access to homes for 40 firemen, a training tower, library, stables, bank and a gymnasium. It also housed a police station and the coroner's court.
Howard Piltz

COVER back
On Ashton Old Road at Pin Mill Brow, Ardwick, in 1964, Ashton BUT 82 on service 218 passes an SHMD Daimler Fleetline inbound on the 21 from Dukinfield. At this junction, the wiring for the former 213 service crossed that for the 218/219, remaining in place for trolleybuses working to and from Hyde Road garage.
Howard Piltz

Frontispiece
The Lord Mayor, Lady Mayoress, aldermen, councillors, general manager and officials pose for the official Opening Day photograph at Rochdale Road garage on 1st March 1938.
GMTS/MCT

First published 2008

ISBN (10) 0 7110 3245 9
ISBN (13) 978 0 7110 3245 3

Published by Ian Allan Publishing

an imprint of Ian Allan Publishing Ltd, Hersham, Surrey, KT12 4RG
Printed in England by Ian Allan Printing Ltd, Hersham, Surrey, KT12 4RG

Code: 0802/B1

Visit the Ian Allan Publishing website at www.ianallanpublishing.com

Introduction

We started this book in 2004, prompted by requests for a new edition of our 1967 'Manchester's Trolleybuses'. During the intervening years, a great deal of additional information has become available, not least the Manchester Corporation Transport Department's vehicle and other records. These revealed corrections to that 1967 book, to our 'The Manchester Bus' and other publications. Rather than an update, we found ourselves undertaking a complete rewrite.

The story of the Manchester trolleybus network is an unusual one. Agitation by vested interests to bring trolleybuses to the city; a Transport Department that did not want them and strenuously resisted their introduction but, when forced to do so, gave the city a system of the highest quality.

Ashton-under-Lyne, which jointly operated the Manchester system, had an earlier trolleybus route which had no bearing on the Manchester network and Ashton (by which title we shall refer to the town in this book) often found itself swept along in Manchester's wake. In complete contrast to Manchester, the other joint operator, the Stalybridge, Hyde, Mossley and Dukinfield Transport and Electricity Board, more usually known as SHMD, wanted to operate trolleybuses but never managed to do so, any plans for a modest fleet being frustrated by the outbreak of war.

The war also caused major changes to Manchester's plans. The need to conserve fuel supplies resulted in the trolleybuses bought for the conversion of the Hyde tram service being used instead to replace motor buses in Moston, bringing trolleybuses to places that not even their most enthusiastic supporters had foreseen.

The vehicle fleet was unusual. Before and just after the war, Manchester City Council's policy of supporting local industry caused the Transport Department to buy most of its buses from Crossley Motors. Based in Gorton, Crossley Motors and its much larger parent company, engine maker Crossley Brothers Ltd, employed many local people. Ashton followed suit but no other trolleybus operator had a large fleet of Crossleys.

Manchester's trolleybuses provided swift, silent and efficient transport for many, the authors included. We hope that this book will continue the role of its predecessor as a worthy memory of them.

Acknowledgements

As with previous books, this has been a team effort. David Beilby, Peter Greaves, Ted Jones, Howard Piltz, Mike Shaw, David Taylor, Peter Thompson and Keith Walker have generously given weeks of their time researching, checking, printing, scanning and tracking down answers to innumerable questions.

Phil Groves kindly updated the chapter he wrote for the 1967 book — we wish that, forty years on, our memories were still as clear and sharp as his. Help with that first book also came from John Miller, Colin Reeve, Arthur Kirby and Ken Swallow, and their contribution is as valuable in 2007 as it was then. In their day the General Managers and staff of Manchester City Transport, the directors and staff of the South East Lancashire and North East Cheshire Passenger Transport Executive and its successor the Greater Manchester Passenger Transport Executive gave us access to all manner of information and answered innumerable questions. Many of those archives are now cared for by the Greater Manchester Museum of Transport from which we had the usual painstaking help from archivist George Turnbull and image curator Mike Shaw. Also as ever, we received generous assistance from the staff of the Manchester City Libraries. The records and library of the Omnibus Society,

the publications of the PSV Circle and the resources of the Kithead Trust were all invaluable. Geoff Burrows kindly provided updates to the technical chapter written for the 1967 book by Fred Eversfield, Manchester Corporation Transport's Electrical Engineer.

Sadly, some friends have passed on. They include our co-author of that first book, Cliff Taylor, who passed away some years ago but not before seeing the realisation of his long-held ambition, the tramway in Heaton Park. Likewise, long-term member of the Transport Department's staff at Queens Road garage, Ray Dunning (whose fine photographs are now cared for by Peter Thompson), Reg Wilson and Arnold Richardson, whose Photobus archive is one of the best in the country. We miss them.

A book of this sort is nothing without its pictures. Many changes have taken place in the city over the past forty years and where possible we have tried to select photographs that show more of the streets than usual. Some of the pictures are less than perfect. Please do not judge the photographers for this; to us it is important to illustrate key events and places even if they were hardly photogenic. We have tried the patience of those who have or care for photographic collections and, as with the research team, the names of the principal

photographers are on the cover page to acknowledge their work. However, the contribution of those who provided a single picture is just as valuable as those who provided dozens. In addition to our collections of pictures taken by Manchester Corporation's staff photographer, the archives of the Crossley family and the Ian Allan Ltd library, we have drawn heavily on the work of Tony Belton, Chris Bennett, C. Carter, Peter Caunt, John Dugdale, Ray Dunning, Don Jones, Ted Jones, John Kaye, Roy Marshall, P. G. Mitchell, Howard Piltz, Arnold Richardson, Peter Thompson, Keith Walker and Reg Wilson. The collections of Chris Bennett and Reg Wilson are now in the care of the On Line Transport Archive ('OTA') whose Charles Roberts and Martin Jenkins kindly spent hours searching for individual pictures. Almost inevitably but certainly unintentionally we shall have missed someone's help or wrongly attributed a picture. To anyone so mistreated we offer sincere apologies.

This book would not have appeared without the support and encouragement of Peter Waller, Alan Butcher and the other members of the Ian Allan team.

To everyone and anyone who helped … thank you.

Michael Eyre, Chris Heaps,
November 2007

The authors and principal contributors are using or gifting their fees for this book for the on-going preservation of our transport heritage, including the Greater Manchester Museum of Transport, the Heaton Park Tramway, other museums concerned with trolleybuses and the various organisations that care for photographic archives.

Manchester Corporation Transport Department never wanted its trolleybuses. Their actual arrival in the city created nothing like the furore that surrounded the question of whether they should be introduced at all.

The city's somewhat capricious interest in trolleybuses started many years before things began to come to fruition. In 1908 the Tramways Committee investigated using either buses or trackless cars, as trolleybuses were then known, for services in the less populous areas where tramcars would not be economic. In a curiously inverted taste of things to come, the Committee decided in favour of trackless cars — and bought motor buses.

Apart from a minor upsurge of interest in 1930 when tramway abandonment commenced in the city, nothing more was heard until 1935. The events of the following months more than made up for the quiet of the preceding decades.

Strongly supported by the Transport Committee and several of the City's Aldermen, the Transport Department's General Manager, Stuart Pilcher, had been pressing on apace with tramway abandonment, using motor buses for the conversions. An extrovert, widely acknowledged as a leader in the transport industry, in addition to his skills in management, leadership and innovation, he was noted for a strong interest in the design and appearance of his buses.

Stuart Pilcher's views on trolleybuses were well known. In an article in the July 1932 edition of *Bus and Coach* he had listed operating costs from eleven trolleybus operators and estimated the cost of operation in Manchester, showing that trolleybuses cost more to build and operate than motor buses. He analysed the labour needed to produce and run the vehicles and the energy required to propel them, proving that, rather than increasing the country's labour force by using home-produced fuel, using electricity actually resulted in employment of fewer people.

He was, therefore, not best pleased when on 3rd April 1935 one Councillor Malcolm urged the Transport Committee to consider operating trolleybuses and to obtain powers to do so. The councillor's motives were seemingly patriotic — use of home-produced coal for power instead of imported oil. There was also a good measure of civic pride, for several other major cities had or were contemplating trolleybuses. However, as with all local government, politics were involved and there were large, powerful local interests in coal. The Lancashire coalfield was in full production, with collieries from Oldham to the concentration of mines around St Helens. Within the city the principal pits were the large, deep Bradford Colliery on Forge Lane, close to Ashton New Road, and the smaller Moston Pit, near Nuthurst Road. Ashton Moss Colliery, better known as the Snipe Pit, was at the boundary of Audenshaw and Ashton-under-Lyne.

On 8th April 1935 the Transport Committee discussed this unwelcome intrusion into their diesel-fuelled realm. The Chairman, Councillor Meachin, reported that the City Council was probably going to instruct the General and Parliamentary Committee to obtain the necessary Parliamentary powers to operate trolleybuses and that it had been suggested that the coming conversion of the Ashton Old Road tram services be deferred until the plan was agreed. Neither Stuart Pilcher nor his Committee saw any virtue in this and decided to replace the Ashton Old Road trams with motor buses as quickly as possible, whereupon an 'electricity lobby' formed and whipped up considerable public support, the Coal Utilisation Council placing large advertisements in the local press extolling the merits of home-produced coal and electricity as opposed to foreign oil.

In the 1930s, power generation was largely in the hands of local authorities, the relatively new National Grid network providing connections between power stations, enabling sharing of load. The Manchester Corporation Electricity Department ('MCED — Heat, Light, Power') was a substantial enterprise, every bit as modern, commercial and professional as the Transport Department. It had large, up-to-date coal-fired power stations at Barton, close to the Ship Canal, and Stuart Street, close to Phillips Park, with smaller ones in the city centre at Dickinson Street and Bloom Street. It also ran a substantial retail business — 'MCED' was the city's prime seller and renter of

Above: Acknowledged as one of the all-time 'giants' of the transport industry, Stuart Pilcher was Manchester Corporation Transport Department's General Manager from 1929 to 1946.
Michael Eyre collection

Left: The cooling towers and chimneys of Stuart Street, one of two large power stations built by the Corporation Electricity Department, dominate this 1953 picture of Ashton New Road with Crossley 1138 bound for the Snipe. The North Road loop ran in front of the row of houses.
Neville Knight

domestic electrical goods. Its offices were to occupy much of the new extension to the Town Hall, then being constructed, on the ground floor of which it had a showroom as large as any of the retail 'white goods' stores of today, complete with lecture theatre and kitchens for cookery demonstrations.

In 1935 MCED generated 642 million kilowatt-hours, 25% of which it sold to the National Grid. Industry consumed 34%, other local authorities supplied by the city 18%, domestic users 15%, trams 6.5% and street lights 1.5%. Profitable demand for its electricity (and hence its usage of coal) was limited only by how quickly it could install new generating plant. The Transport Department's consumption of electrical power was relatively unimportant to the Electricity Department, the more so as it had to be supplied at cost, and its management team may well have welcomed the decrease in the Transport Department's need as a result of tram conversions.

Not unexpectedly, support came from the joint operators that would be involved. Ashton-under-Lyne Corporation was enthusiastic — it already ran a small number of elderly trolleybuses on a service to Hathershaw and had a modestly sized electricity generating station in Wellington Street. The quaintly named Stalybridge, Hyde, Mossley and Dukinfield Tramways and Electricity Board ('Tramways' was changed to 'Transport' in 1936) ran no trolleybuses but wanted to. SHMD, as it was known, generated electricity at its modern Hartshead Power Station, between Stalybridge and Mossley. Its earlier Tame Valley Power Station in Park Road, Stalybridge, closed down in 1932 but remained as a tram and bus depot.

On 1st May 1935 the City Council rejected the Transport Committee's plan to use motor buses for the Ashton Old Road conversion. Irritated, the Transport Committee resubmitted their proposal on 31st July. The Council again rejected it, this time by a majority of only seven votes. It decided to promote the Parliamentary Bill and instructed the Transport Committee to maintain the tramcars on Ashton Old Road until the Bill was passed.

Stuart Pilcher responded to this snub of his professional advice with dignity and determination, proposing a temporary service of motor buses, no doubt hoping that this could become permanent. The Council replied bluntly *'that it was no solution and that it was high time that Manchester experimented with the trolleybus'*.

In December 1935 the introduction of the Parliamentary Bill was agreed. Powers were sought to run trolleybuses over the whole of the Department's operating area subject to the consent of the relevant local authorities — the operating area extended well beyond the city boundaries — and were specifically obtained for Wythenshawe and Trafford Park. The conditions were *'as if the apparatus and equipment for working the trolley vehicles were tramways and as if the trolley vehicles were carriages used on the Tramways'*.

Publication of the Bill brought some objections. Oldham and Salford were opposed to trolleybuses as was the Society of Motor Manufacturers and Traders because it did not prohibit the Corporation from manufacturing its own vehicles — adjacent to its Hyde Road garage the Transport Department had a large and comprehensive bus and tram overhaul works (the 'Car Works') where it built a substantial number of new bus bodies. As expected, Ashton and SHMD supported the Bill but there was less relevant backing from elsewhere. Heywood, for example, was many miles from the proposed route but its council stated that it would not oppose use of trolleybuses in the town.

Suitable protective clauses were negotiated with Oldham, Salford, Ashton, Bury, Stockport and Altrincham, and the Bill was approved by the Committee On Unopposed Bills on 14th May 1936. The trolleybus would come to Manchester.

A reluctant Transport Committee started planning. On 1st July 1936 the Committee asked the Council for authority to buy land for a garage in Rochdale Road. This was referred back for an investigation into the suitability of part of the former Lancashire and Yorkshire Railway Carriage Works in Thorp Road, Newton Heath — a location that would have involved miles of empty running.

Exasperated, Stuart Pilcher prepared a comprehensive and thorough report in which he showed that the cost of the 43 trolleybuses, plus overhead wiring and equipment, would be £112,306 (£4million in 2007 money values), whilst 43 motor buses would cost only £86,000 (£3million). Armed with these facts, the Transport Committee had another go at the City Council, as did the Electricity Lobby. At the 31st July 1936 Council Meeting the Transport Committee's proposal to buy motor buses for Ashton Old Road was defeated by 69 votes to 33 and the Department was instructed to use trolleybuses. It was, however, given permission to buy the Rochdale Road site for the garage.

The Council also ordered the Committee to give up its plan to use part of the site of Gaythorn Gas Works (on Medlock Street, behind the railway between Knott Mill and Oxford Street) for daytime city-centre bus parking, a cost-saving scheme which would have avoided buses having to run back empty to the garages in the suburbs after the morning rush hour, and vice versa in the evening. The Department had also considered using it for trolleybuses and the Transport Committee had authorised leasing of the site from 1st July 1936. The whole idea had to be abandoned.

Above: In the mid-1930s anything electric was 'modern' and its growing use was an important factor in the lobbying for trolleybuses. The Corporation Electricity Department was as commercial and enterprising as the city's Transport Department; this is the advertisement for its new showroom in the Town Hall Extension, opened in May 1938, shortly after the trolleybus system.
Michael Eyre collection

Below: SHMD was equally active in promoting the use of its electricity. This advertisement appeared in the SHMD bus timetable.
Michael Eyre collection

This 1946 picture captures police concerns about potential congestion from trolleybus dewirement. Imagine what would happen if Leyland 1032 was to dewire as it crossed Piccadilly from Portland Street to Newton Street en route to Rochdale Road garage, having completed its morning rush-hour turn on the 31x from Fairfield Road. The guard stands on the platform, ready to jump off and pull the frog for Newton Street. The Transport Department's head office, 55 Piccadilly, is the dark-coloured building on the left. Leyland TD5 810 is going back to Parrs Wood garage, its indicators partly wound off from service. Crossley 'Standard' 549 and Streamliner 735 are arriving on limited stop service 8 from Hyde. Bogie tram 924 and a 'Pilcher' car wait for 1032 to cross.
Peter Thompson/MCT

Stuart Pilcher and the Transport Committee tried new tactics. If the Ashton Old Road service was to be converted then would it not be wise to convert the parallel Ashton New Road service also? They managed to prolong the discussion on the conversion until 3rd March 1937, almost two years after the argument had started, when the Council, after some indecision, agreed to include the Ashton New Road service. It might have gone the other way in which case the vehicle order could easily have been changed to motor buses.

On 24th November 1936, whilst recommending to the Council that it replace the Cheetham Hill trams with buses, the Transport Committee suggested somewhat pointedly that the tramway poles should be left in place *'so that trolleybuses could be introduced at a later date if the Council feel it desirable'*. This time the Council did not.

Much later, Stuart Pilcher set down his personal views in the April 1939 edition of the industry magazine *Bus and Coach* to which he was a regular contributor: *'Some amount of agitation was raised during the several months when the Manchester conversion report was under consideration, by the action of organisations representing electricity and coal. Advertisements were displayed in the newspapers, members of the City Council were canvassed and public meetings were convened. A less pleasant side of local government service is experienced in having to counter the activities of persons free from the responsibilities of office, yet agitating for a particular line of policy in face of the considered opinions of those most familiar with local circumstance.'* He went on to express the view that the Coal Lobby was more interested in the effect Manchester's decisions would have elsewhere rather than in any cost savings for the city itself. It says much for his status and the respect in which he was held by all that this article provoked no comment from the City Council.

The Ashton New Road tram services to be converted to trolleybuses were the 26 (Stevenson Square — Ashton-under-Lyne) and cross-city 27 (Droylsden — Old Trafford). On Ashton Old Road the services were the 28 (Piccadilly — Ashton-under-Lyne) and cross-city 31 (Fairfield — Chorlton). Although the Transport Department was not enthusiastic to do so, the 26 and 28 would be extended to Stalybridge, involving the SHMD Board in addition to Ashton-under-Lyne, and the latter two would erect and maintain the overhead and electrical equipment in their respective areas.

In forcing through the trolleybus system the City Council had ignored major issues that would stifle the development of the trolleybus system. Since the days of horse buses, the police had had strong concerns about the congestion caused by trams and buses in the centre of the city, and this had caused the splitting of the cross-city express bus network introduced in the late 1920s. Their views had not changed. Fear of the chaos resulting from dewirements meant that trolleybuses would not be allowed into the heart of the city — Market Street and Deansgate in particular. They would have to terminate on the edge of the city centre, depositing passengers some distance from the principal shopping and business areas.

These objections also affected cross-city services, which had long been shown to be popular and to produce higher revenue. Such services had to use the city centre streets but the police objection meant that their operation with trolleybuses would not be allowed. The 27 and 31 would have to be split and only their eastern sections converted to trolleybuses.

Owing to the decision to convert

Tram   Services

to

Bus and Trolley Bus Operation,

alterations may be made in the near future.
Notification of these changes will be posted up
in all Trams and Buses.

MCT

The cost of the overhead wiring, with new poles only where needed to support extra weight, was estimated at £8,506 (£0.3million in 2007 money). It would turn out to be more than this, for Stuart Pilcher had determined that if the Corporation wanted a trolleybus system then it would pay for the very best that could be obtained. It got precisely that, a fine system with top-class overhead, the best quality equipment, the most modern vehicles in the country and a splendid purpose-built garage. Opposed to it he may have been but Stuart Pilcher was a true professional and gave the city a system of which it could be proud.

Tenders were invited for the supply of 23 six-wheel and 23 four-wheel trolleybuses, with bodies to the Department's standard 'Streamline' design. The following tenders for bodywork were received:

Firm	6-wheel	4-wheel
Leyland Motors Ltd	£1,035	no quote
Cravens Railway Carriage and Wagon Co Ltd	£1,037	£960
Crossley Motors Ltd	£1,090	£995
Metropolitan-Cammell-Weymann Motor Bodies Ltd	£1,090	£995
English Electric Co Ltd, Bradford	£1,090	£995
English Electric Co Ltd, Preston	£1,090	£995
Brush Electrical Engineering Co Ltd	£1,090	£995
Park Royal Coachworks Ltd	£1,090	£995
Charles H. Roe Ltd, Leeds	£1,090	£995
Strachans Successors Ltd	£1,152	£1,092
F. D. Cowieson & Co, Glasgow	£1,600	£1,500

Although against the law in 2007, this sort of price fixing by manufacturers was normal at the time. In the case of buses it was intended to help a general manager select his supplier on engineering grounds and experience, avoiding his being forced into 'lowest price' decisions by councillors. Price negotiations took place after suppliers had been chosen.

Contracts were actually placed for 76 vehicles, sufficient for the Ashton New and Old Road services. In line with its policy of supporting industry within the city, the City Council's preferred supplier of buses was the Gorton firm of Crossley Motors Ltd, subsidiary of the larger Crossley Brothers Ltd, based in Openshaw, close to Ashton Old Road. This had been the subject of a previous bitter dispute between the City Council and the General Manager, who in 1929 and 1930 had been forced to cancel orders for a fleet of Leylands and AECs and, until such time as the council agreed otherwise, buy Crossleys and a smaller number of Leylands.

In 1937, however, Crossley's two modestly sized Gorton works were fully loaded, with large orders for military lorries in addition to those for corporation motor buses. With time of the essence, although the instruction to buy Crossleys stood, the Transport Department was purchasing an increasing number of Leylands. The trolleybus chassis order was divided accordingly, Leyland receiving an order for 36 (10 four-wheel chassis and 26 six-wheel), whilst Crossley's share was 40 (28 four-wheelers and 12 six-wheelers). The correct term for the respective types of vehicle is 'two-axle' and 'three-axle' but the Transport Department always called them 'four-wheelers' or 'six-wheelers' and these terms are used in this book.

The order for bodywork went to Crossley, incorporating the Department's usual requirement for use of Metropolitan-Cammell's all-metal body framing. Placing the whole contract with Crossley was to prove an embarrassment on opening day — Crossley was late delivering.

Because of the very high torque that an electric motor can deliver, a trolleybus chassis has to be somewhat different from that of a motorbus. In addition to the mountings for motor and resistances, the rear of the frame must be made stronger and the differential and axles more substantial. Crossley Motors had already built two prototype trolleybuses in a serious but fruitless attempt to win some of London Transport's orders. Before starting it had realised it needed proven experience and had therefore headhunted the Chief Designer from the Sunbeam Trolleybus Company Ltd of Wolverhampton. The two prototypes later became Ashton 49 and 58. Both had bodies using a London-style frame. Thus, the firm was well placed to do the work and by 13th November 1937 had completed eight Manchester vehicles, one of which was taken to Glasgow to be exhibited at the Scottish Commercial Motor Show the following week. They were tested on Ashton's Hathershaw route and delivered to the newly completed Rochdale Road garage on 5th December.

Crossley's first prototype trolleybus was a six-wheeler. Built in 1936 for a bid to win orders from London Transport, its body had a London-style Metro Cammell frame and followed London practice in having the trolley base over the third bay of the body.
Ian Allan Library/Crossley Motors

Manchester's Crossleys 1000-1007 were completed during November 1937 and tested on Ashton's Hathershaw route, where 1006 was photographed before going for display at the Scottish Commercial Motor Show in Glasgow. The overhead wiring of the Hathershaw route was of an older type, requiring temporary fitting of trolley wheels instead of carbon sliders. In contrast to the London style, the trolley base is neatly panelled over and blended into the roof line. The large octagonal objects on the roof house are suppressor chokes; a Crossley patent to prevent radio interference, it proved an overkill.
Ian Allan Library/Crossley Motors

The trolleybuses were numbered in a new series starting at 1000, well away from the buses then being numbered around 650. The reason was to allow following bus drivers to recognise a trolleybus and avoid one trolleybus attempting to overtake another. By 1941 the bus fleet numbers had overtaken the trolleybuses and the method was no longer effective, instead a white 'O' (for 'overhead') was painted on the lower off-side rear corner of all Manchester trolleybuses. That the vehicles were unusual for Manchester was further emphasised by their having long blocks of consecutive registration numbers — at that time the city's motor taxation office, (unusually) operated by the police, would only allocate registration numbers for buses as and when each one was ready for service. The new vehicles turned the scales at 7tons 9cwts 1qr (four-wheel) or 9tons 2cwts (six-wheel), their electrical equipment making them considerably heavier than their diesel counterparts.

The Department's staff erected the poles and overhead wiring to the highest standards. The wire was supplied by Richard Johnson and Nephew Ltd, a substantial cable manufacturer with a works in Forge Lane, opposite Bradford Colliery. Electrically the system had an odd feature in that the city centre section was isolated from the rest and supplied directly from Dickinson Street Power Station. The majority was fed from existing electricity substations, using underground cables installed for the tramways. Feeders to the overhead wiring were about one mile apart, each having a rectangular pillar-box sized green-painted iron cabinet set in the pavement.

The overhead wiring raised the question of 'tower wagons' to erect and service it. Previously the Department had converted old buses for this task and several solid-tyred veterans were still at work. Having forced through the trolleybuses, the Council could hardly reject the Department's proposal to buy three modern purpose-built Thornycrofts.

In March 1937 the builders moved onto the site in Rochdale Road, about a mile from the city centre. Costing £55,000 (a similar building would cost circa £5million in 2007 money) plus £22,000 (circa £2million) for the land, the excellent 45,000 sq ft garage area accommodated 115 vehicles. It had up-to-date sunken maintenance bays, the most modern equipment that could be obtained, exceptionally comprehensive facilities for the staff and could handle anything except major overhauls, which would be done at the Car Works. Even the main garage doors were of an advanced electrically operated all-steel folding design. There was also the Department's usual fire station-like bay for the Overhead Equipment Department's tower wagons, fitted for a fast turn-out complete with fast-opening folding doors and slippery pole from the staff accommodation on the first floor. Intended for the new Thornycrofts, this emphasis on speed of departure was somewhat marred by one of the bays being occupied by a 1919 solid-tyred AEC converted from a bus in the 1920s.

To make sure that all was ready for the Ministry of Transport inspection, the Transport Committee took a trip along Ashton Old Road to Beck Street, Fairfield on 25th January 1938 using Leyland 1064. This greatly pleased Leyland Motors, which sent along its photographer. 1064 had not dewired; the bus was slewed across the road for the photograph, traffic light enough for this to be done without fuss. Its trolley booms have had to be moved to the inwards track because the trolleybus wires had been temporarily carried above the tram wires. An Ashton Corporation tram on service 28 waits. New Thornycroft tower wagon DXJ 97 was also on show.
Ian Allan Library/Leyland Motors

The system went live on 4th January 1938 and on the 25th members of the Transport Committee took a trip along Ashton Old Road as far as Fairfield Road on six-wheeler 1064. Although they passed close to Crossley Brothers' works, 1064 was a Leyland and the firm took full advantage of this opportunity for publicity. Overhead construction in the city was completed in February and on the 22nd and 23rd Major Wilson, the Ministry of Transport's Inspecting Officer, examined 1007, 1051 and 1068 and approved routes and vehicles for use. As well he might, for the whole system was of the highest quality. The vehicles were the most up-to-date in the country and of smooth, modern appearance, the full-width front enhancing the looks of the Department's 'Streamline' body style. Design and styling was important in Manchester's buses and a subtle touch was the rear profile of the bodywork, which curved gently inwards, matching that of the front — the rear of the motor buses had an outward flare. Opening Day was set for 1st March.

However, things had not gone quite so smoothly as might seem from the above. In January it became clear that, due to illness and shortage of materials, Ashton's overhead wiring was not going to be completed in time for the Major's inspection. Given the argument over introduction of the trolleybuses, this could not be allowed. The Manchester overhead line crews brought out their stocks of equipment, loaded up lorries and tower wagons, drove to Ashton and by 8th February had put up the wiring from Chester Square to St Michael's Square. Ashton paid.

There were problems at Gorton too, where Crossley was behind schedule. In mid February it was clear that by opening day Crossley would deliver only half of the 46 trolleybuses required to operate the full peak-hour Ashton Old Road service. There would be ten four-wheel Crossleys (1000-1009), two six-wheel Crossleys (1051/52) and eleven six-wheel Leylands (1062-1072).

The politics were such that the opening could not be postponed and Stuart Pilcher devised an ingenious solution. The trams would run in the morning, the formal inauguration would take place at about mid-day at Rochdale Road garage and the civic party would then go by trolleybus to Piccadilly, where as each service 28 tram arrived it would be replaced by a trolleybus for the next journey from Manchester; likewise at Ashton which shared operation of the service. Having watched the first two or three changeovers, the party would go swiftly (ironically by motor bus) to a celebratory civic luncheon at the Town Hall in Albert Square, well away from the trolleybuses. By the time the evening rush hour arrived and trams reappeared to cover for the missing trolleybuses, the civic group would have departed homewards, replete with food and wine.

On schedule at mid-day on 1st March 1938, the Lord Mayor, Alderman J. C. Grime, performed the opening ceremony at the new garage, Stuart Pilcher looking on with a benign smile. The Lord Mayor, aldermen, councillors, officials and guests then boarded trolleybuses and went to Piccadilly, where they gave the first in-service trolleybus a suitable civic send-off just before 1pm, moving on to the Town Hall for lunch. In his speech Stuart Pilcher commented that the price of electricity at 0.73 pence/unit was far too high and that if Electricity Departments wished to encourage the trolleybus they would have to reduce their prices. The trolleybus in Manchester, he added, would be given a fair trial.

The progressive changeover outside rush hour had avoided the embarrassment of drawing attention to the vehicle shortage. It would have needed a very knowledgeable guest to notice how few vehicles there were in Rochdale Road garage. There was good reason for Stuart Pilcher's smile.

Crossley did not miss its target by much, delivering a further 21 during March — four-wheel Crossley 1021, four-wheel Leylands 1028-1037 and six-wheel Crossleys 1050/53-1061. The rest of the 76 arrived during April, May and June and were stored in the garage until the Ashton New Road services commenced on 1st August 1938.

The principal Ashton Old Road trolleybus service took the tram service number (28) and was operated by Manchester and Ashton vehicles. It ran from a city terminus on Portland Street, at the end of Piccadilly Gardens (Manchester vehicles showing Piccadilly on their destination blinds) via Ashton Old Road to Ashton-under-Lyne and Stalybridge. When it started, the Stevenson Square — Ashton New Road — Ashton tram service 26 was cut back to the Ashton boundary at the Snipe Inn, adjacent to Ashton Moss Colliery (better known as the Snipe Pit), enabling the end of tramcar operation in Ashton.

The Lord Mayor, Alderman Joseph Grime MBE, makes the opening speech. Stuart Pilcher looks on, smiling benignly.
MCT/Michael Eyre

Inside the new Rochdale Road garage on opening day. The garage was as empty as it looks for only half the required vehicles had been delivered. Crossley 1003 and Leyland 1064 are on the pits.
MCT/Michael Eyre

Lacking its front bumpers, Crossley 1005 turns from Aytoun Street into Portland Street, returning from one of the first runs to Stalybridge.
MCT/Ian Allan Library

Until sufficient vehicles had been delivered, particularly six-wheelers to handle the rush-hour loads, trams 31 and 31A continued to run to Fairfield, ending on 19th March 1938. On Monday 21st, they were replaced by all-day trolleybus services 29 from Piccadilly to Audenshaw Road, The Trough and Fairfield Road (29x) but rush-hour trams to Fairfield Road and Bessemer Street had to continue, the last ones running on Maundy Thursday, 13th April, before the Easter weekend. The delay also caused some irritation to the City Engineer whose department was waiting to resurface the roads.

The intention for the southern half of tram 31 was that it would be converted to motor buses and extended to Levenshulme, replacing some of the Stockport Road trams, as cross-city motor bus service 88 (Chorlton — Seymour Grove — Deansgate — Market Street — Levenshulme). This was scheduled for June of 1939, there being more pressing priorities for new motor buses to be used elsewhere. In the interim the Levenshulme — Exchange tram (37) was extended to Chorlton. The war then caused further postponement — the 88 started in August 1946 running between Exchange and Chorlton but delays in the delivery of new buses meant that the long-planned extension to Levenshulme did not

start until October 1949 (bus 94).

Things went smoothly for the Ashton New Road conversion, where the last trams ran on 30th July 1938, trolleybuses taking over the following day. This time the conversion aroused considerable interest and crowds gathered to watch the final car, in marked contrast to the end of the trolleybuses twenty-eight years later.

The principal Ashton New Road trolleybus service was numbered 26, ran from Stevenson Square to Stalybridge and, although strictly a joint service, was operated only by Manchester, as had been the case with the trams. Short workings ran all day to the Snipe (27) and Edge Lane (27x). Trolleybuses terminating at the Snipe reversed into Gainsboro Road (sic) using a newly installed turning 'Y'.

When the 26 commenced on 31st July, the all-day service 29 journeys along the Old Road to The Trough were extended to the Snipe and renumbered 28x, service 29 to the Trough then only running at rush hours. The all-day 29x to Fairfield Road continued.

Like the 31, the 27 tram had run cross-city and the loss of this facility caused concern. The seemingly curious solution, said to be based on traffic demand, was a new bus service numbered 83 which followed the route of the 27 tram from

Warwick Road (Trafford Park at rush hours) via Stretford Road, All Saints and Piccadilly, to a strangely isolated terminus at Adair Street on Great Ancoats Street. Adair Street was between Pollard Street (trolleybuses outwards) and Every Street (trolleybuses inwards) where any cross-city passengers could easily change buses. In fact the plan was that when the trolleybus issue had become less controversial, the 83 motor bus would become a full cross-city service, extended at its southern end to Firswood (which started in 1939) and, at its northern end, along Ashton New Road, North Road and Edge Lane to Clayton Bridge, running every 15 minutes. War delayed the latter until 1946.

Trolleybuses there might be, but important full time cross-city links from both Ashton roads had been severed. Almost. For without notice or debate, motor buses quietly replaced the rush-hour trams from Higher Openshaw to Trafford Park (29x, March 1938) and Droylsden to Trafford Park (27x, December 1938); a 28x was added in the 1960s. Still showing these former tram service numbers, they continued to run into the days of the SELNEC Passenger Transport Executive, long after the trolleybuses had gone and almost every other bus service had been renumbered.

Trolleybus services, November 1938

26	**Stevenson Square — Ashton New Road — Audenshaw — Ashton — Stalybridge**
26x	Stevenson Square — Ashton New Road — Audenshaw — Ashton
27	**Stevenson Square — Ashton New Road — Audenshaw, Snipe**
27x	**Stevenson Square — Ashton New Road — Droylsden, Edge Lane**
27x	Stevenson Square — Ashton New Road — Clayton, North Road
28	**Piccadilly — Ashton Old Road — Audenshaw — Ashton — Stalybridge**
28x	Piccadilly — Ashton Old Road — Audenshaw — Ashton
28x	**Piccadilly — Ashton Old Road — Audenshaw, Snipe**
29	Piccadilly — Ashton Old Road — Audenshaw Road, The Trough
29x	**Piccadilly — Ashton Old Road — Higher Openshaw, Fairfield Road**
29x	Piccadilly — Ashton Old Road — Openshaw, Grey Mare Lane
Services shown in light type were rush-hour or part day	

Above left and right: The new trolleybuses bore very little external indication of their maker. There was a circular 'Crossley' transfer on the front panel of those with a Crossley chassis but the only indication of the maker of the Leylands was on the wheel hubs. Crossley 1055 and Leyland 1063 at Rochdale Road garage in March 1938. There was a shortage of trolleybuses on Opening Day and the urgency to deliver resulted in some of the normally-chromium-plated front bumpers having to be painted; others arrived without them.
Crossley Motors

Right: Although Ashton's new trolleybuses may seem somewhat plain by comparison with Manchester's stylish Streamliners, they represented what was orthodox in bus design at the time and proved as durable as the Manchester vehicles, running until 1956. Leyland 52 at bodybuilder English Electric's works in Preston.
English Electric via David Beilby

Left: This picture shows the full set of destination indicators on the rear of the 1000-series — the 'intermediate' indicator blinds on the back and the side destination and intermediate blinds were all taken out of use during and after the war. The white 'O' (for 'overhead') on the rear corner was added during the war to warn drivers of following trolleybuses not to attempt to overtake. The red-painted rear dome was introduced on the trolleybuses because the cream domes became stained with water drips and black dust from the trolley booms. Leyland 1034 in Stevenson Square, October 1955.
Michael Eyre

Right: For opening day Ashton had two new Crossley six-wheelers which, minor details apart, were the same as Manchester's. This is fleet number 46 in 1948, showing the signs of a long stint of wartime use. Manchester Leyland 1120 and the Crossley behind illustrate how the streamline livery evolved, the upper-deck swoops being given up in 1945 just before Stuart Pilcher retired and the lower-deck ones when Albert Neal succeeded him in 1946.
C. Carter/Ian Allan Library

Gallery — The Stalybridge services

Stevenson Square
Right: Looking towards Newton Street, shows the square in March 1943. The photographer must have taken a considerable risk as any wartime photography was certain to attract suspicion. Leyland six-wheeler 1084 on the 26 is drawing on to the stand; behind is 1073 on a 27x.
George Lawton/Omnibus Society Library

Edge Lane, Ashton New Road
Right 1327 leaves the Edge Lane 215x terminus to run back to the city. The picturesque half-timbered building is the Transport Department's traffic and parcels office. October 1964.
Peter Thompson

Ashton New Road, Droylsden
Right: At Market Street junction, Droylsden, 1357 passes a policeman waiting to help a group of people cross the road safely. Williams Deacon's Bank is on the near corner of Market Street and beyond it are the offices of Droylsden UDC, which looked more like a church than a council building. June 1966.
Peter Thompson

Grey Mare Lane, Ashton Old Road
Lunchtime on Tuesday 11th May 1965, on Ashton Old Road just east of Grey Mare Lane, Openshaw, and with the turn-back wiring from Ryder Street on the right of the picture, 1322 works a 218x to Audenshaw. The two corner shops are plastered with cigarette advertising and a mother has left her baby in a pram outside one of them — something that one would hardly contemplate in 2007.
Peter Thompson

Ashton Old Road, Higher Openshaw
Audenshaw-bound 1357 on Thursday 1st April 1965. The Alhambra Cinema was a notable local attraction in Higher Openshaw; Redman's grocers occupied part of the building and their 'self service' stores were something of a novelty at the time. The day was unusually warm and sunny, and the shops have their sunblinds out.
Peter Thompson

Fairfield Road
A hundred yards further along Ashton Old Road, Ashton 85 pulls away from a line of heavy traffic that has stopped at the Fairfield Road traffic lights. The sunblinds are out once more and the shops display their wares on the pavement. June 1963.
Peter Thompson

Fairfield Wells
At Fairfield Wells terraced housing gave way to sizeable Victorian and Edwardian villas. On 9th April 1965 en route to take up service on the 127, long converted from trolleybus 217, the crew of Leyland-bodied Leyland PD2 3339 has stopped for a brew at the Department's Fairfield traffic and parcels office, which was in one of the adjacent shops. City-bound on the other side of the road, Ashton's Bond-bodied BUT 86 picks up passengers.
Peter Thompson

The Trough
The Stalybridge and Guide Bridge services divided at the Trough: 28s (later 218s) to the left, 29s (later 219s) to the right; 31s (later 29x, 219x and 212) turned back. The horse trough and its cistern pillar are at the apex of the junction. 1307 inbound and 1311 outbound on 8th September 1963.
Peter Thompson

The Snipe
At the Snipe, trolleybuses reversed into Gainsboro Road, using the only 'turning Y' on the network.
'Trolleybuses must not stand in this road' reads the Department's warning sign ... ... but they did. Leyland six-wheeler 1079 in 1955.
Ray Dunning

Ashton Market Place
Bow Street, alongside Ashton's open-air market, was the terminus of the 216x, 217, 218x and 219. There was an overhead siding so that Stalybridge-bound 216s and 218s could pass. This is maker BUT's picture of new Ashton 85. The market was not in full swing that day with only the fruit and vegetable stalls in action; the funfair, too, was closed. Behind it can be seen the roof of a former Manchester Corporation double-deck Crossley, converted to a showman's vehicle. An Ashton Leyland PD2 stands outside the Town Hall in the right background.
Ian Allan Library/BUT

Stamford Street and Old Street
A ticket inspector waits in Old Square, Ashton, for Manchester-bound 1357. The wiring from Ashton Market Place terminus joins from the left of the picture. Yates's Wine Lodge was a long-established Lancashire chain that, for many years, in addition to alcoholic beverages also sold fresh beef reared by the Yates family on their Cheshire farms. December 1966.
Peter Thompson

Stamford Park
Having enjoyed the sunshine in Stamford Park, at half past four on a warm Saturday afternoon a crowd waits to board 1308. Situated across the boundaries of Lancashire and Cheshire, and Ashton and Stalybridge, the park takes its name from the Earl of Stamford who, along with a local mill owner, gave the land to the two towns. June 1962.
Peter Thompson

Thompson Cross
At Thompson Cross, trolleybuses turned off Stamford Street and descended Rassbottom Street to Stalybridge town centre. Ashton 84 is followed down the hill by a Ford Thames Trader tipper. The cross was named after religious poet Francis Thompson who lived at 226 Stamford Street, Ashton, where there is a blue plaque to his memory.
Peter Thompson

Rassbottom Street
1357 in Rassbottom Street on a sunny day in May 1966 with a background of the hills of Longdendale. To the right is Stalybridge station, famous for the pub on its platform. Still open for travellers and townspeople to enjoy a pint, a cup of tea or a meal, the Station Bar dates back to 1885 and retains many of its original features.
Neville Knight

Stalybridge
The postwar six-wheelers rarely appeared on the Stalybridge services. Before pulling onto the Town Hall loading stop, 1247 waits outside the former SHMD Head Office in Waterloo Road at 4.30pm before what would become a busy rush-hour journey. Built in 1904, the SHMD offices passed to the North Western Electricity Board in 1956. Much later they were converted to flats and renamed Thorn House, the doorway's carved and dated SHMD capstone being carefully retained. . Friday 21st August 1959.
Peter Thompson

A Big Red Bus
When Stalybridge Bus Station opened, the one-way loop round the town centre was reversed, trolleybuses leaving the town via Waterloo Road. The bus shelter and its sign capture SHMD's functional down-to-earth style — the shelter panels are rusting away and the sign reads confusingly — *'Ashton, Droylsden, Clayton, Manchester, Lower Mosley Street , No 6, Hurst Cross, Pitses, Oldham, No 8.'* The latter had another designation: Oldham service N. There is no mention of the much more frequent trolleybuses, although their numbers appear on the stop flag. It didn't matter; the locals knew what stopped where. 1347 bound for Stevenson Square in June 1962.
Peter Thompson

Three

Expansion

The Ashton Old Road (28 and 29) services' city terminus was on Portland Street, at the 'far end' of Piccadilly Gardens. Well away from Market Street, it was opposite the then Queens Hotel and in full view of Stuart Pilcher's office in the MCT headquarters at 55 Piccadilly. The route into the city was via Fairfield Street and Aytoun Street; outward buses turned right into Piccadilly/London Road, passing the railway station but keeping the trolleybuses at the edge of the city centre. Provision was also made for turning some rush-hour trolleybuses even further short of the centre by a loop from Fairfield Street into Whitworth Street and back to London Road.

On the 'Old Road' there were turning loops ('turn-backs') back to Manchester at Grey Mare Lane (Ryder Street), Dakeley Street, Fairfield Road (Beck Street) and The Trough. The first three used narrow side streets with wiring on bracket suspension arms and were difficult to negotiate. That at Dakeley Street was so tight that six-wheelers could not use it and it was removed after a few weeks; it was almost opposite the steel works in Bessemer Street where rush-hour trams had reversed for both Manchester and Ashton. Ashton trolleybuses turned there by reversing into Bessemer Street on their batteries — unlike many systems, all the Manchester and Ashton's modern vehicles (other than the latter's wartime deliveries) had traction batteries, which enabled the bus to move slowly without overhead power for a moderate distance.

In Audenshaw the roads to Ashton and Guide Bridge divide at The Trough where the road was wide enough for a turning circle. 'The Trough', incidentally, was exactly that. At the apex of the road junction there was a splendid granite drinking trough for cart horses; one of many installed across the country by the Metropolitan Drinking Fountain and Cattle Trough Association which was still in existence and active in 2007. Inscribed 'A righteous man regardeth the life of his beast', the trough was still in place at the time of writing although used for a flower display.

The city terminus of the 26 and 27 Ashton New Road services was also on the edge of the city centre in Stevenson Square. Here again there was a one-way system for trolleybuses — outward via Hilton Street and Oldham Street to Great Ancoats Street; inward along Newton Street and Hilton Street. There were intermediate turning points at North Road, Clayton and Edge Lane, Droylsden, where the Department had a Traffic and Parcels Office.

The Old and New Road routes joined at the Audenshaw/Ashton boundary near the Snipe Inn and Ashton Moss Colliery. Up to this point both roads were ideally suited to trolleybuses — straight and densely populated with frequent stops. The Ashton system started with a further straight level section across Ashton Moss to Chester Square, where the town of Ashton starts. Famous for its market gardens and celery, Ashton Moss had few houses and was the scene of some high-speed running.

The narrow streets of Ashton required further one-way working, the route dividing at Henry Square, outwards from Manchester via Old Street and inwards via

Above: The Trough' was precisely what its name implied — a horse trough. One of many installed across the country around the turn of the century by the Metropolitan Drinking Fountain and Cattle Trough Association, it is inscribed '*A righteous man regardeth the life of his beast*'. Two people sit on the bench around the cast iron pillar containing the trough's water supply cistern, which has the appearance of a French '*pissoir*'. 1322 and 1321 on the 218 in June 1965. *Peter Thompson*

Left: If a Manchester vehicle failed in Ashton's operating area or Stalybridge, Ashton would provide a changeover and vice versa, which would sometimes bring an Ashton vehicle onto the New Road. In July 1955, with a Manchester crew in charge, Ashton 60 waits to draw onto the 216 stand in Stevenson Square. Leyland 1115 behind is on the 211 to Moston. *Roland Scott via Peter Thompson*

Stamford Street, with the terminus in Bow Street alongside the market — the detail is shown on the map. Beyond Ashton, at Stamford Park the route crossed into Cheshire and the operating area of the Stalybridge, Hyde, Mossley and Dukinfield Transport and Electricity Board. Approaching Stalybridge on a clear day upper-deck passengers had fine views of Mottram Moor and the hills of Longdendale. The final section into Stalybridge was a steep descent of Rassbottom Street, passing the railway station, famous for the licensed pub on its platform. There was a clockwise terminal loop via Waterloo Road, with the setting down point outside SHMD's offices, and Market Street, with the picking up point outside the Town Hall.

Joint trolleybus operation in Britain was uncommon. An unusual feature of the Manchester network was the reciprocal arrangement for the changeover of defective trolleybuses. Should, for example, a Manchester vehicle develop a serious fault in Ashton, it would be replaced by an Ashton vehicle and vice versa, vehicles being re-exchanged at the first opportunity. Thus from time to time one could see a vehicle of either operator standing in the other's garage or in service with one of the other operator's crews. The indicator blinds on Ashton vehicles therefore included displays for the Stevenson Square services on which Ashton did not normally work.

Such changeovers could be welcomed by the crews, as in the following tale. Sometime in the 1960s a Manchester vehicle failed in Ashton on the Stevenson Square service (by then numbered 216) and its crew was duly provided with a blue Ashton vehicle. Everything was normal to the Snipe but thereafter the crew were surprised when waiting passengers stood back and let them pass. They quickly worked out the reason. It was a blue Ashton bus and the only Ashton vehicles that normally worked on the New Road were motor buses on the 6 (Glossop) service — a limited stop that charged higher fares. They carried almost no one; life was easy. Looking forward to a repeat of this good luck for the rest of their turn, the crew were greatly disappointed on arrival at Stevenson Square to find a Hyde Road fitter waiting with a replacement Manchester vehicle.

Shortly afterwards fate took revenge on that same crew. They were at Ashton working the final journey of the day, leaving just before 11pm when their Manchester vehicle failed. They phoned Ashton's garage for a changeover but the phone was unanswered — Ashton's staff had gone home. Our disgruntled heroes had to wait an hour for an equally unimpressed Manchester recovery team to

come out from Hyde Road and rescue them. Next day Ashton received a memo reminding it of its responsibilities.

Returning to the events of 1938, the Department still had no wish to extend the trolleybus system and in a comprehensive report proposing the final abandonment of the tramways, Stuart Pilcher noted that *'there are certain other routes where trolleybuses could be operated but in considering these routes regard should be paid to the higher cost of operation of the trolleybus'.* These were tram services 19 (Victoria Street — Denton — Hyde), 33 (Victoria Street — Belle Vue — Reddish), 34A (Piccadilly — Belle Vue) and 51 (Miller Street — Ardwick — University), bus 57 (Ashton — Denton — Haughton Green, jointly operated with Ashton and a tram service until November 1936) and bus service 15x (Piccadilly — Guide Bridge). Once again, the Council ignored his advice and ordered the Transport Committee to convert them all to trolleybuses apart from the section of the 33 from Bull's Head, Reddish, to Houldsworth Square and Vale Road — a slightly pointless action as this portion was in the Borough of Stockport and outside their jurisdiction.

Inclusion of the 15x demonstrated the contrived nature of the situation. It interworked with cross-city bus 15 (Guide Bridge — Piccadilly — Worsley) which was jointly operated with Salford. Nevertheless, the 15x would become trolleybus operated whilst the 15 would continue to be worked by motor buses.

If the City Council now thought that it had won the war with its Transport Department it was soon to find that it was wrong. When it became apparent that the trolleybus battle was not going his way, Stuart Pilcher determined to force through the abandonment of the remainder of the tramways in one single action. How he achieved this, cleverly turning the Council's cancellation tactics to his advantage, is beyond the scope of this book. Suffice it to say that after much to-ing and fro-ing and some perilously close voting, Stuart Pilcher won the day and his plan received the approval of the City Council on 1st February 1939. His only concession was

that the trolleybus proposals were adopted. The conversion involved buying 550 new motor buses and 77 new trolleybuses, at a total cost of around £1.3million (some £50million in 2007 money).

The trolleybus contracts were for 37 four-wheelers from Leyland with English Electric bodies (1100-1136) and 40 four-wheelers from Crossley with Crossley bodies on the usual Metropolitan-Cammell frames (1137-1176); 44 were for the Hyde Road service but no six-wheelers were included. Ashton ordered eight Crossley four-wheelers to the same design. The massive orders for motor buses were spread more widely to ensure delivery — chassis by Leyland, Daimler and Crossley, bodies by Crossley and English Electric, for the quantities were far beyond that which Crossley Motors could build.

Back on the ground, as it were, the mile or so of overhead from The Trough along Audenshaw Road to Guide Bridge for the 15x conversion was swiftly completed by the Department's staff and on 16th October 1939 the all-day trolleybus service to Fairfield Road (29x) was extended to Guide Bridge, replacing the 15x motor bus and using vehicles from the existing fleet. Short workings to The Trough and Fairfield Road were renumbered 31 and 31x.

It made obvious sense to extend the 29 to Ashton, using wiring that Ashton would be installing for the conversion of the 57 (Haughton Green — Ashton) bus from Guide Bridge, joining the 26 and 28 routes at Chester Square, Ashton. This was quickly done but extension of the 29 service had to await delivery of new vehicles, delayed by the start of the war. It was extended to Ashton on 22nd March 1940, Ashton sharing its operation, 29x then being used for the Guide Bridge short workings.

Compared with what was to come, the 29's delay was but a trivial hitch. The war was about to cause major changes to the plans. The unwelcome trolleybuses would play an important part in saving imported oil and providing an efficient service on some of the city's busiest routes on which their operation had never been contemplated.

Trolleybus services, March 1940

26	**Stevenson Square — Ashton New Road — Audenshaw — Ashton — Stalybridge**
26x	Stevenson Square — Ashton New Road — Audenshaw — Ashton
27	**Stevenson Square — Ashton New Road — Audenshaw, Snipe**
27x	**Stevenson Square — Ashton New Road — Droylsden, Edge Lane**
27x	Stevenson Square — Ashton New Road — Clayton, North Road
28	**Piccadilly — Ashton Old Road — Audenshaw — Ashton — Stalybridge**
28x	Piccadilly — Ashton Old Road — Audenshaw — Ashton
28x	**Piccadilly — Ashton Old Road — Audenshaw, Snipe**
29	**Piccadilly — Ashton Old Road — Guide Bridge — Ashton**
29x	Piccadilly — Ashton Old Road — Guide Bridge
31	Piccadilly — Ashton Old Road — Audenshaw Road, The Trough
31x	Piccadilly — Ashton Old Road — Higher Openshaw, Fairfield Road
31x	Piccadilly — Ashton Old Road — Openshaw, Grey Mare Lane

Services shown in light type were rush-hour or part day

Above: Just beyond the Trough, towards Guide Bridge and close to Aldwyn Park Road, there was a short stretch of almost open country as the road approached the bridge over the Woodhead electric railway line. On a sunny September day in 1963, Ashton 84 is Manchester-bound on the 219. The overhead has an unusual arrangement of bracket arm with triple spacer to hold the curve.
Peter Thompson

Above right: The 219 route then skirted Manchester Corporation Waterworks' huge Audenshaw Reservoirs. 1330 is at Lumb Lane, where the inwards stop had an elegant brick and tile shelter set beneath the bank of the reservoir. This area was much changed by the M60 motorway.
OTA/Reg Wilson

Above: The small radius of the Guide Bridge turning circle had to be negotiated with care. Its indicator changed for the return journey, 1202 is about to turn back to Manchester. Behind, 1337 will go straight on to Ashton.
Peter Thompson

Left: Having joined at the Snipe, the 216 and 218 routes crossed Ashton Moss and entered the town of Ashton at Chester Square; the 217 and 219 came in from the right of the picture. The Byzantine-style tower in the background is that of the former Ashton-under-Lyne municipal public baths.
Peter Thompson

Four

Disruption

For any contract concerned with the defence of the realm, the government can stipulate that it take precedence over civil work. It did so at Crossley Motors which was increasingly involved in the production of military vehicles. The firm received orders for over 2,000 military trucks (it would build over 10,000 during the war) and bus production for Manchester slowed in consequence, such that the trolleybuses due for the October 1939 conversion of the 15x bus did not start to arrive until the following February. A similar situation applied to the Leyland and English Electric vehicles. The 29's extension to Ashton, conversion of tram 51 (University), motor bus 57 (Haughton Green) and tram 19 (Hyde) had to be delayed — by ten years in the case of Hyde.

The 51 route skirted the northern and eastern edges of the city centre. Starting at the junction of Corporation Street with Miller Street (near Victoria Station) it crossed Rochdale Road, Oldham Road, Ashton Old Road (at Pin Mill Brow) and Hyde Road (at Ardwick Green) to a terminus in Brunswick Street, close to Manchester University on Oxford Road. The majority of this was already wired for trolleybus working with existing overhead between Rochdale Road and Ashton Old Road, and along Chancellor Lane which was wired for access (via Devonshire Street North) to Hyde Road works and garage.

Deliveries of the new trolleybuses commenced in February 1940. Sufficient had arrived to allow the 51 tram to be withdrawn on 23rd March, a temporary bus service operating whilst the tram overhead in Higher Ardwick and Brunswick Street was replaced by trolleybus wires. Trolleybuses took over on 5th April. The service was renumbered 30 but the major changes to the plans to be recounted later in this chapter meant that equipment could not be spared for the short length along

Miller Street to Corporation Street and the initial terminus had to be on existing wiring at Thompson Street, just off Rochdale Road and about 200 yards from the garage, with a one-way loop round Swan Street and Rochdale Road. At the University the terminus was just short of Oxford Road at New York Street, where there was a turning loop through side streets.

Next to be tackled was the 57 Haughton Green service. Wiring was completed from Guide Bridge to Denton; Ashton and Manchester trolleybuses took over on 1st July 1940, a Manchester 57x motor bus shuttling thence to Haughton Green. Bombing raids on the city then caused completion of the wiring to Haughton Green to be delayed.

The service number was unchanged, although it was altered to 17 in July 1947. This seemed strange, clashing as it did with the trunk 17 Manchester — Rochdale motor bus service. It was in fact an Ashton-under-Lyne Corporation series number and the reason for the change was that hitherto Ashton's trolleybuses had not displayed service numbers but were being fitted to do so. The blinds had been ordered with the number 17 rather than 57 and Ashton did not wish to alter them.

Given its much larger size, one might have expected Manchester to overrule to this but service numbers were never Manchester's strongest point. Bus service numbers duplicated those of trams running on quite different services. The trolleybuses

were a curious mixture of the two series and subject to frequent changes. Such was this ambiguity that at one stage an unsuspecting passenger would find buses, trams and trolleybuses in the city centre all showing the same service number but headed for widely different destinations, and for some years there were instances of different bus services with the same number running in widely different parts of the city. All this was in stark contrast to the precision of the Engineering Department and probably reflects the difference in priorities of the two.

With the arrival of Crossley 1138, Rochdale Road garage had reached its designed capacity of 115 vehicles and 1139-1162 were delivered to Hyde Road garage, which added them to its existing total of around 200 motor buses and tramcars, the plan being that it would operate the Hyde service.

The worsening of the war brought restrictions on the use of fuel oil and this caused major changes to the trolleybus system. Unwanted it might have been but it was now to come into its own as a means of conserving precious supplies. Several tram services were reinstated and the Hyde Road tram-to-trolleybus conversion was halted — little work had been done because of the impending crisis. The Hyde trams would continue and the new trolleybuses and equipment ordered for it would be used to save diesel fuel by converting two heavily trafficked motor bus services.

Delivery of the 1100-series trolleybuses commenced in February 1940, delayed by the start of the war. This is 1136 before delivery from English Electric, Preston. The rear and side indicator displays were simplified on the second type of Streamliner body.
English Electric via David Beilby

SHMD also stopped work, having installed the turning loop along Newton Street, George Street and Clarendon Street, near Hyde Market Place. After the war, this became an oddity for it was never used or connected to the rest of the system because of the decision to extend the Hyde service to Gee Cross. Nevertheless, this wiring remained in place until 1956 — providing a source of puzzlement and speculation.

In 1935 SHMD had given up working its trams, by then somewhat run down, on the 19 service, Manchester taking over its operation. However, it seems there were thoughts of sharing operation of the Hyde trolleybus service for, although there is no formal record, there are indications that it may have made some informal arrangements with the Sunbeam Trolleybus Company Ltd, Wolverhampton, for chassis with bodies by Northern Counties, Wigan, SHMD being listed as a client in a contemporary Sunbeam publicity brochure. The delay in the Hyde conversion caused these to be cancelled, if they ever existed. After the war and taking into account the impending nationalisation of electricity generation, SHMD decided it did not wish to own trolleybuses. It was agreed that Manchester would continue sole operation, buying extra vehicles for the extended service. The result was that the closest SHMD ever came to a trolleybus was with its overhead-equipment maintenance tower wagons.

In the city, the obvious choice for unplanned trolleybus conversion were two heavily trafficked motor bus services that passed the trolleybus garage on Rochdale Road — service 60 (Church Street — Rochdale Road — Victoria Avenue — Cheetham Hill Rd — Cannon Street) as far as Blackley Estate on Victoria Avenue, and the 55 (Church Street — Rochdale Road — Conran Street — Moston, Ben Brierley — Chain Bar, Gardener's Arms), together requiring just over 40 buses at peak times. The 'Ben Brierley' was a pub at the corner of Moston Lane and Kenyon Lane, named after a Lancashire dialect poet. The adjacent area was known as 'The Ben'.

To free up sufficient space at Rochdale Road, the main duties on services 28, 29, 30 and 57 would be moved to Hyde Road, which commenced trolleybus operation on service 30 in April 1940 and the 57 on 1st July, sharing their working with Rochdale Road.

A legal snag was then discovered. The Moston via Rochdale Road tramway had ended at Hall (later Hillier) Street at the foot of Sankey's Brow on Moston Lane, just beyond Conran Street. The Moston via Oldham Road tracks reached The Ben via Kenyon Lane and beyond the Ben along Moston Lane terminating at Moston (St Joseph's Roman Catholic) Cemetery. No powers were available under the existing

Acts of Parliament for Moston Lane beyond Hall Street to The Ben and from Moston Cemetery to Chain Bar. There was no time for a Parliamentary Bill to be promoted and in May the General Manager wrote to the Chief Inspecting Officer of Railways, Lieutenant-Colonel Mount, who replied that the work could be done under Emergency Orders, provided the Corporation undertook to obtain the required powers in due course. The Corporation would have to take full responsibility for the work, Stuart Pilcher personally certifying that he had inspected it, that weight limits on bridges were obeyed and that the electrical arrangements were acceptable to the General Post Office (which was responsible for the telephone system at the time) and that he would comply with any requirements made when things were legalised.

This is not a superb shot but it is a significant one. 1123 is just south of Central Avenue (later Harpurhey Road), Harpurhey, on part of Rochdale Road which would have been served by the 60 conversion. This 214 has worked out on the evening peak via Conran Street and is running back to Church Street for another journey. Although its blinds are set and the service number appeared on the stops, a trolleybus was unlikely to stop for passengers on this section of Rochdale Road. 23rd April 1955, the last day of operation of the 214.
Ted Jones

Work started in June 1940 and proceeded briskly. Stocks of poles were limited and the fittings obtained for Hyde Road would have to suffice for the overhead. Fortunately, many of the former tramway poles had remained in place for street lighting. The electrical supply seemed good with suitable feeder points at Rochdale Road garage, Queens Road and Blackley.

There was then a further setback. Wiring along Rochdale Road for the Blackley service was well in hand, points (correctly 'frogs' or 'turn-outs') had been fitted at the corner of Moston Lane and Rochdale Road,

ready for the wiring of the Blackley service, and 'Blackley Estate' had been added to the destination blinds when, to the Department's dismay, a major technical snag was discovered. The electricity network in Blackley was insufficiently robust to withstand the high peak demands of the trolleybuses. The plan had to be reconsidered.

Fortunately, there was surplus power and the necessary supply infrastructure on the route to Moston via Oldham Road, where the Moston (24) tram service had been converted to cross-city bus 80 (Moston — Chorlton) in 1938. Instead of the Blackley Estate service, the Moston via Oldham Road section of bus 80 could therefore be converted. There was concern whether the stocks of equipment would now be sufficient to reach beyond Nuthurst Road to Charlestown Road (80) or Chain Bar

(55). In fact, the only shortfall was the need for some poles, which were obtained by removing alternate ones from the tramways in Great Western Street, Lloyd Street, Moss Lane East, Raby Street and Boston Street, Moss Side, where the wiring became slack and performed spectacular oscillations when trams passed.

The Luftwaffe then intervened. Flushed with the success of victory in France, it turned its attention to targets in Britain and began attacks on Manchester. On 1st September 1940 trolleybus 1081, outward bound along Fairfield Street, was badly damaged by blast and splinters from a

nearby bomb explosion. Defiantly, 1081 was back in service in a month, repaired and fully repainted, streamlines and all, but this damage was only a small foretaste of things to come.

Intense bombing on 8th October caused severe devastation, in particular on Rochdale Road, Collyhurst. For several weeks all buses (trams had long gone from Rochdale Road) had to be diverted at Queens Road, reaching the city via Cheetham Hill Road or Oldham Road. There was no question of any trolleybuses to Moston until the buildings were made safe and the road and new but unused trolleybus overhead repaired.

Worse followed. On 23rd October the Rochdale Road, High Street, Miller Street and Cannon Street areas of the city centre were blitzed, damaging more of the new and unused trolleybus overhead. Several city bus termini had to be temporarily relocated. Bus services 55 and 60 were moved to terminate in Stevenson Square so that bus services 16 (Heywood) and 17 (Rochdale) could use the terminus in Church Street. The overhead line crews had to leave their new wiring to repair the damaged tram and trolleybus overhead. The blitz continued. It was July 1941 before the city centre roads and wiring were repaired, damaged buildings either made safe or demolished and the rubble cleared, allowing the buses to return to their normal termini.

A great patriot, Stuart Pilcher was not one to be stopped by the activities of the Luftwaffe. As soon as the debris in Collyhurst had been cleared, the Rochdale Road trolleybuses would start, reaching the city by using the existing wiring from the garage and the Stevenson Square terminus. Diversion of the overhead line crews to

repairs meant that the new overhead in Moston was finished only as far as the junction of Upper Conran Street with Moston Lane. No matter, fuel had to be saved and from 4th November 1940 the trolleybuses took over the high frequency rush-hour journeys to Moston Lane, running round the Rochdale Road, Moston Lane, Upper Conran Street, Conran Street loop clockwise numbered 60x and anti-clockwise numbered 55x, motor buses continuing to operate the journeys on 55 beyond Upper Conran Street.

Completion of the 57 service wiring to Haughton Green was similarly delayed. It came into use on 9th December 1940, saving more diesel fuel. The overhead construction gang also finished the wiring along Moston Lane to the Ben Brierley and the trolleybus service was extended there in January 1941; the six stops beyond The Ben to Nuthurst Road were served by motor buses on soon-to-be converted service 80. This provided an opportunity for the Department's Traffic Section to show that it, too, was not perturbed by the Luftwaffe by indulging in some service renumbering. The Moston service became 32 and displayed the extraordinary destination 'Ben Brierley'. Short workings to Moston Lane/Conran Street continued, numbered 60x or 32x respectively.

The Rochdale Road route had one section of unusual wiring. This was at the long skew bridge at Reather Street, just beyond the garage, that carried Rochdale Road over the main line railway from Victoria station en route to Newton Heath and beyond. It was not possible to plant poles on the bridge with the result that the overhead spans, supported from either end of the bridge, were very long. The roadway rose about two feet as it crossed the railway

and trolley booms had to dip accordingly; the speed for trolleybuses across was therefore limited to fifteen miles per hour. The Department placed a speed limit sign to this effect at both sides of the bridge but this was often ignored with no ill effects — wartime restrictions there might have been but Manchester's overhead was still to the highest standards.

On the nights of 22nd and 23rd December 1940, Manchester experienced a major blitz. The city was terribly damaged, the night sky bright with flames. Fortunately the operational trolleybus system was not in the worst hit area and damage was confined to overhead near Mayfield station and at Rochdale Road/Thompson Street which was quickly repaired on a temporary basis. When permanent repairs were carried out, the opportunity was taken to revise the city centre power arrangements. Until this time the supplies for trams and trolleybuses had been separate with 'dead' sections everywhere tram and trolleybus overhead intersected. Apart from the supply anomaly and the disruption caused if a vehicle stopped with its trolley on an insulated section, these dead sections gave rise to frequent blue flashes if a vehicle crossed with power on; drivers were supposed to coast across them but this was not always possible in busy traffic. These flashes were deemed by the government to be easily visible to the Luftwaffe, passing on their less lawful journeys above, and the Air Ministry asked all tram and trolleybus operators to take steps to reduce them. This was an excellent opportunity to rationalise the power supplies. It was speedily done and at the same time hoods were fitted over the turn-outs, cross-overs and section gaps.

The white roofs of the buses were conspicuous, especially when parked in groups at night. They were therefore painted grey — something that was continued after the war with the introduction of 8ft wide buses to assist garage staff setting up the new bus washing machines — grey roofs for 7ft 6in wide buses, red roofs for 8ft wide buses. Also, water drips and black carbon powder from the trolley heads stained the white rear domes and on the trolleybuses these were painted red at overhaul.

Portland Street 1939
Crossley 1016 approaches the stand for the Ashton Old Road services. The line of 'nose in' parked cars was a feature until the 1950s. To the right is the bus station; officially 'Parker Street' but everyone called it 'Piccadilly'. Behind are the offices and warehouses of cotton spinners Barlow & Jones Ltd, makers of the famous 'Osman' towels ('*just hug you dry*') and Sparrow, Hardwick & Co Ltd, equally famous for its 'Sparva' fabrics, shirts and bed linen.
MCT/Michael Eyre

Portland Street 1940
Although Leyland 1076's roof has not been painted all-over grey, other preparations for the war are evident — concrete air raid shelters have been built in Piccadilly Gardens and a brick blast wall erected on the pavement in front of the entrance to the Hollins Mill Company building, outside which the tram has stopped. Two taxis stand at the rank in front of the bus and in front of them is J. Rice & Sons' ice cream cart.
MCT/Ted Jones

Portland Street 1941
The Barlow & Jones Ltd, Sparrow, Hardwick & Co and other buildings have been flattened by the December 1940 blitz. Concrete air raid shelters have been built on Piccadilly Gardens, the burnt-out buildings cleared and contractors, using a steam crane and traction engine, are levelling the site and building more air raid shelters. Leyland 1082, bound for Ashton on service 29, has had its roof painted grey and headlamps masked. The parked cars are still there, for fuel shortages had not yet reached crisis proportions.
MCT/Michael Eyre

As a further fuel-saving measure, on 10th March 1941 the 15 cross-city bus from Guide Bridge to Worsley was split at Piccadilly, its eastern section being covered by extra journeys on trolleybus 29x.

Repairs done, the overhead crews' next task was to ad trolleybus wiring to the tram overhead in Oldham Road and erect poles and wiring along Thorp Road, Lightbowne Road, Dean Lane (later Kenyon Lane) and Kenyon Lane to the Ben Brierley. From 27th June 1941 some journeys on service 80x between Stevenson Square and the Ben Brierley were operated by trolleybuses. Ironically the Thorp Road section passed the part of the former Lancashire and Yorkshire Railway Carriage Works that the City Council had considered acquiring for the trolleybus garage.

On 14th July 1941, the 16 and 17 buses moved back to Cannon Street, allowing bus 60 and trolleybus service 32 to move to their intended terminus in Church Street, working in via Shudehill and out via Oldham Street. In Moston the wiring was completed as far as Nuthurst Road and on the same day the Moston via Oldham Road trolleybus service replaced the northern half of the 80 (Charlestown Road — City — Chorlton) motor bus service. Hyde Road

garage took over many of the duties on the Ashton Old Road (28/29/31) services, receiving ten Leyland six-wheelers (1062-1071) from Rochdale Road to add to 24 new four-wheel Crossleys (1139-1162). Six-wheelers were not used on the Moston services because they could not safely negotiate the tight corners at Upper Conran Street and Thorp Road; four-wheelers 1163-1171 went to Rochdale Road to balance the transfer of 1062-1071. The fleet now stood at 148 vehicles, 114 at Rochdale Road and 34 at Hyde Road, with 1172-1176 still in build at Crossley's Gorton works.

The Stevenson Square to Moston via Oldham Road service was numbered 37. For the next three weeks until the overhead was completed to the Gardener's Arms, where there was a suitable turning place for the trolleybuses at the Victoria Avenue

MANCHESTER CORPORATION TRANSPORT DEPARTMENT

CHANGES IN CITY TERMINI

Commencing on Monday, 14th July, the Heywood and Manchester Bus Service No. 16 and the Rochdale and Manchester Bus Service No. 17 will operate to and from CANNON STREET instead of Church Street. These services will run outward via Miller Street and inward via Withy Grove.

The Town Terminus of the "Ben Brierley" and Stevenson Square Trolley Bus Service No. 32 will be changed to CHURCH STREET.

SS, Piccadilly, Manchester, 1. 5th July, 1941.   R. STUART PILCHER, General Manager.

MANCHESTER CORPORATION TRANSPORT DEPARTMENT

MOSTON AND CHORLTON BUS SERVICE No. 80 CONVERSION TO TROLLEY BUS OPERATION

Commencing on Monday, 14th July, the Moston (Nuthurst Road) and town portion of the above route will be operated by trolley buses. The town terminus will be Stevenson Square and the service number 37. Trolley Buses terminating at the "Ben Brierley" on this service will be numbered 37x.

During morning, evening and Saturday noon rush periods a connecting motor bus service will run between Elaine Avenue and Nuthurst Road. This service will be a temporary one pending conversion to trolley bus operation beyond Nuthurst Road.

The Chorlton and Piccadilly portion of No. 80 service will continue to be operated by motor buses and Piccadilly loading point will be near Aytoun Street (Portland Street).

Starting and finishing times on these services will be as at present.

SS, Piccadilly, Manchester, 1. 5th July, 1941.   R. STUART PILCHER, General Manager.

Michael Eyre

roundabout, a motor bus ran a shuttle service (numbered 80x) to Charlestown Road and Chain Bar.

On 2nd August the trolleybus services were extended to the Gardener's Arms, and were renumbered again — service number changes were something that Moston residents would have to learn at more or less regular intervals. Gardener's Arms via Oldham Road became 36, with rush-hour shorts to Ben Brierley as 37. The Rochdale Road service remained 32, the all-day journeys to the Ben were numbered 33 and the rush-hour Moston Lane/Conran Street shorts were all numbered 33x, running in via Conran Street in the morning and vice versa in the evening. The 'in via Conran Street, am only' short workings sometimes showed 34 — this became general in 1948.

As previously mentioned, it did not seem to matter that there were bus, trolleybus and tram services with the same number in the city centre — bus 33 to Romiley, trolleybus 33 to Ben Brierley and tram 33 to Reddish. After the war, the Department had motor bus services numbered 17 (Cannon Street — Rochdale), 26 (Moston via Crumpsall), 31 (Piccadilly — Bramhall) and 34 (Stevenson Square — Oldham) which duplicated trolleybus services, although service numbers 25 and 35 were not used for trolleybuses, presumably

Above: Bright sun makes Stevenson Square look somewhat more appealing than it was. This centre island on the Newton Street side of Lever Street was added in 1948 to ease congestion and was used by the Moston via Oldham Road service. 1009 and 1112 on the 211, behind them, Oldham Corporation's Roe-bodied Leyland PD2 360 is going to Waterhead on service 98.
P. G. Mitchell

Left: There was not much attractive about the trolleybus terminus in Church Street and it was rarely photographed. This picture also shows a little of the bomb damage in the High Street and Shudehill area that caused postponement of the start of the Moston trolleybuses. The corner site behind the bus was a victim; as with many of the blitzed sites it remained undeveloped for many years, hidden by advertisement hoardings. 1006 on 22nd April 1955.
Ted Jones

because by some logic it was thought important to avoid a clash with buses 25 (Stevenson Square — Newton Heath) and 35 (Cannon Street — Bury). In the Manchester series there were also motor bus services numbered 27, 28, 29, 30, 32, 36 and 37 but, although the Transport Department had an interest, these were operated solely by the North Western Road Car Co Ltd, Stockport.

A rush-hour variation of the 55 was not sufficiently frequent to convert to trolleybuses. This turned off Conran Street to run half a mile along Church Lane to Holmfield Avenue. Numbered 55x, it continued to run with its 'orphaned' motor bus series number.

Also on 14th July 1941, the all-night motor bus service to Clayton and Snipe was replaced by trolleybus 27x which ran from Stevenson Square to the Snipe, outwards along Ashton New Road, returning via Ashton Old Road.

The revised plan had been carried out efficiently, with great speed and little disruption. Whatever bad feelings there

were from the events of the Coal Lobby, everyone could be proud of the achievements in Moston.

On 23rd August 1943, a short extension was opened from the Gardener's Arms along Greengate to the private bus station built to serve the A. V. Roe & Co Ltd aircraft factory, busy turning out Lancaster bombers and other aircraft, and services 32 and 36 ran there at rush hours. The last 200 yards of this was outside the city boundary and in the Urban District of Chadderton, although still within the Department's operating area. It was built under a further Emergency Order. Crossley's bus production had been halted in 1941 and the last five of the new trolleybuses (1172-1176) were stored part-built in its Gorton works. Their completion during 1942 and 1943 was sanctioned to enable the A. V. Roe extension to be opened. Although there were stringent rules about the design and finish of wartime vehicles, the Crossley staff cheerfully ignored them and painstakingly completed 1172-1176 to full prewar

standards, with polished chromium plate, varnished woodwork, deep moquette and leather seats, full indicator displays and streamline livery — the justification being that all the necessary parts, materials, fittings and paint were waiting in the stores. The fleet then reached its planned strength of 153.

Ironically, the need to conserve coal supplies then led to economies in the use of electricity, the situation becoming particularly acute in the winter of 1943/44. To save power, tram (the city had 364 trams in service) and trolleybus services were reduced and several of the numerous request stops were removed — and in many cases never reappeared. During the war years staffing difficulties brought lady guards ('clippies') and also 'auxiliary guards' — regular passengers who had volunteered to supervise loading, ring the bell, and call out stops. In Manchester no lady bus or trolleybus drivers were appointed, although there were some lady tram drivers. Ashton did have lady conductors and this gave rise to a subtle

Right: Even with the increase in private motoring, the AVRO bus station continued to be busy in the 1950s and 1960s. Leyland 1103, a motorbus and another 1100-series Leyland are on the 211/212.
Neville Knight

Below: In 1943 a short extension was added beyond the Gardener's Arms, along Greengate to the Chadderton aircraft works of A. V. Roe and Co Ltd, busy building AVRO Lancaster bombers. This picture, taken in 1946 from the first floor offices, shows 12 trolleybuses and 28 motor buses, new and old and some in wartime red and grey livery, waiting in the private bus station to take workers home to all parts of the city.
MCT via Michael Eyre

difference between the two operators' working practices. The guard (Ashton used the more usual title of conductor) normally dealt with poling and de-poling the trolley booms. However, the springs which hold a trolley boom against the wires are very strong and whilst a man, being generally of heavier weight and strength, could manoeuvre them using the bamboo pole, there was a real risk that a smaller, lighter female conductor could be lifted off the ground and in a mixed Ashton trolleybus crew it was the driver's task.

The legal niceties were tidied up in the Manchester Corporation Act of 1946 which included a section entitled 'Trolley Vehicle Powers' which formalised the two Emergency Orders under which the Moston routes had been constructed.

Powers were also obtained in this Act to construct a short spur from Edge Lane, Ashton New Road, along Manor Road and Chappell Road to Sunnyside Road. This was to be subject to agreement with the very independent A. Mayne & Son Ltd, which operated the service along this route and also one from Dale Street in the city centre along Ashton New Road to Kershaw Lane, Audenshaw (just short of the Snipe) which competed directly with the 26 and 27 trolleybuses. Such competition is normal in 2007 but then was most uncommon, and Arthur Mayne and the Transport Department were, to put it mildly, never the best of friends. Not surprisingly, Mayne's approval was never given and only in 1957 did Mayne and the Corporation reach agreement on jointly operated bus service 46 from Stevenson Square to Sunnyside Road.

Trolleybus services, 1946

26	**Stevenson Square — Ashton New Road — Audenshaw — Ashton — Stalybridge**
26x	Stevenson Square — Ashton New Road — Audenshaw — Ashton
27	**Stevenson Square — Ashton New Road — Audenshaw, Snipe**
27x	Stevenson Square — Ashton New Road — Droylsden, Edge Lane
27x	Stevenson Square — Ashton New Road — Clayton, North Road
28	**Piccadilly — Ashton Old Road — Audenshaw — Ashton — Stalybridge**
28x	Piccadilly — Ashton Old Road — Audenshaw — Ashton
28x	**Piccadilly — Ashton Old Road — Audenshaw, Snipe**
29	**Piccadilly — Ashton Old Road — Guide Bridge — Ashton**
29x	Piccadilly — Ashton Old Road — Guide Bridge
29x	Piccadilly — Ashton Old Road — Audenshaw Road, The Trough
29x	Piccadilly — Ashton Old Road — Openshaw, Grey Mare Lane
30	**Rochdale Road — Ancoats — Ardwick Green — University — Greenheys, Platt Lane**
31x	Piccadilly — Ashton New Road — Higher Openshaw, Fairfield Road
32	**Church Street — Rochdale Road — Moston, Ben Brierley — Moston, Gardener's Arms**
32x	Church Street — Rochdale Road — Moston, Ben Brierley — Moston, Nuthurst Road
33	**Church Street — Rochdale Road — Moston, Ben Brierley**
33x	Church Street — Rochdale Road — Moston Lane
36	**Stevenson Square — Oldham Road — Moston, Ben Brierley — Moston, Gardener's Arms**
36x	Stevenson Square — Oldham Road — Moston, Ben Brierley — Moston, Nuthurst Road
37	Stevenson Square — Oldham Road — Moston, Ben Brierley
57	**Ashton — Guide Bridge — Denton — Haughton Green**
57x	Ashton — Guide Bridge — Denton
57x	Ashton — Guide Bridge

Services shown in light type were rush-hour or part day

Above right: Ever a thorn in the Transport Department's flesh, A. Mayne & Son Ltd of Clayton ran a fast service along Ashton New Road from Kershaw Lane, just short of the Snipe, to Dale Street, one block towards Piccadilly from Stevenson Square, and it had a loyal following. Arthur Mayne's buses were as different from the Corporation's as could be. Almost all were AECs, finished in a distinctive maroon and pale blue livery, with a green light at the side of the destination box to help passengers identify them at night. This 1955 picture is of 1936 AEC Regent CNB 1 which was fitted with a new East Lancashire body after the war, of similar pattern to its original Park Royal.
Ted Jones

Right: The start of the evening rush on Wednesday 29th April 1959: a queue waits to board Mayne's East Lancashire-bodied 1949 AEC Regent KNA 877 at the Dale Street terminus.
J. S. Cockshott Archive

Gallery —
The University service

Thompson Street
The need for overhead equipment for emergency conversion of the Moston services forced a change in the initial terminus of the 30 to a somewhat isolated stop on the existing wiring in Thompson Street, by the blank rear wall of Oldham Road goods station. In this May 1959 picture of 1317 turning from Rochdale Road into Thompson Street, the original terminal stop few yards ahead of it.
Peter Thompson

Oldham Road
At the other end of Thompson Street, the route turned right into Oldham Road then left into Great Ancoats Street at the busy New Cross junction. Notable in this picture, looking up Oldham Road from New Cross, is Mason's Square Deal Stores. Behind Mason's was Sanitary Street, later tastefully renamed Anita Street — a change that the City Surveyor's Department effected with ingenious economy by simply removing letters S, R and Y from the first word on the existing street sign. The dual carriageway is marked by substantial cast iron bollards, which Health and Safety Regulations would not allow in 2007. 1305 bound for Greenheys in May 1959.
Peter Caunt

Adair Street
On Great Ancoats Street in 1946, two passengers wait for a 30 at the Adair Street stop. The man in the raincoat looks hopefully at the approaching trolleybus but 1175 is on a 27x to Edge Lane and is about to turn left into Pollard Street. The signage is typical 1930s MCT — an oval bus stop flag (yellow and black for stops, red and white for fare stages) with separate frames for service numbers and queuing instructions.
MCT via GMTS

Ardwick Green
After the war, six-wheelers were used on the service to carry crowds to and from matches at Manchester City's Maine Road ground, although in this 1959 picture, in Higher Ardwick, 1240's passengers are mainly lady shoppers.
P. G. Mitchell

Brunswick Street
From the Ardwick Green roundabout BUT 1335 turns into Brunswick Street, passing a Standard Vanguard stopped awkwardly on the pedestrian crossing whilst its driver talks to someone on the pavement. Behind the bus is Hyde Road. Paul Anka is to star at the Ardwick Hippodrome. June 1959
Peter Caunt

University
Carrying football fans back from Maine Road in 1959, 1253 is near the initial 30 terminus at New York Street, with Oxford Road and the original Manchester University buildings in the background.
P. G. Mitchell

Market Street, Ashton
Ashton and Manchester shared operation of the Haughton Green service, and the former's contribution on 30th April 1949 included English Electric-bodied Leyland 55, new in 1937. It was followed along Market Street, Ashton, by 1936 Crossley Mancunian 24 (ATJ 895) which also had an English Electric body.
Roy Marshall

Ashton Market
The 217 terminus in Ashton was Market Place, where there was a siding allowing trolleybuses bound for Stalybridge to pass services terminating at Ashton. 1332's paintwork shows signs of wear above the windscreen — there was a problem with flaking paint on several of the Burlingham bodies, some having to be repainted after only two years. June 1959.
OTA/Chris Bennett, Martin Jenkins

Guide Bridge
At St Stephen's Parish Church, Guide
Bridge, the 217 turned left into Guide
Lane, to pass over the railway at Guide
Bridge station. The bus stops were
thoughtfully arranged so that
passengers would board a Manchester-
bound 219 outside the church beyond
the roundabout and thus not miss the
short workings turning back at Guide
Bridge. 1320 in June 1959.
OTA/Chris Bennett & Martin Jenkins

Audenshaw boundary
1332 crosses the Audenshaw/Denton
boundary. As with the Old and New
Roads, there was a short stretch of
modern semi-detached houses but the
majority of the route was intensely
urban.
OTA/Chris Bennett & Martin Jenkins

Ashton Road, Denton
Ashton Road, near Annan Street,
Denton, in 1951. Ashton 59 has just
passed the Hyde and Denton Equitable
Co-operative Society's stores. Next door
is the Silver Springs pub; towards Crown
Point are the Co-op clothes shop,
Walker's ironmongers and White's
tobacconists. There are no cars and the
scene looks calm and uncluttered
compared with today. Although the
adjacent area was much changed by the
construction of the M67 motorway and
the more recent Denton Retail Park,
almost all the buildings in the picture
remained in 2007.
Omnibus Society Library/Ted Jones

Crown Point
Left: Short workings to Denton on 217x turned at Crown Point. Buses would cross Hyde Road and then go left round the side streets onto Hyde Road and turn right back to Ashton. The Cheshire-registered Mercedes Benz 220 car dates from 1957 — although 'Mercs' are familiar today, they were rare in the UK in the 1950s. 1320 in June 1959.
OTA/Chris Bennett & Martin Jenkins

Stockport Road
Below left: On Stockport Road, Denton, looking back to the Carter's Arms and almost at the junction with Two Trees Lane, Ashton Crossley 'Empire' 77, going to Haughton Green, passes a parked 1952 Standard Vanguard and is followed by a 1954 Standard 10. June 1959.
Peter Caunt

Haughton Green Road
Above: The approach to Haughton Green was along the quiet, tree-lined Haughton Green Road with the terminus at what was then quite literally the end of the road. The sun reflects off 1332 as it approaches the terminus.
OTA/Chris Bennett & Martin Jenkins

Haughton Green
Left: Ashton 49, the Crossley four-wheel prototype, at the Haughton Green terminus on 30th March 1956. The clock is a 'Bundy' time recorder into which the guard would insert and turn a key to record the departure time. Later replaced with Time Recording Co's clock-card systems, the clocks were much disliked by the crews; they were given up in 1967 having become impractical with the general introduction of one-man buses.
Roy Marshall

Five

Recollection
Philip Groves

During 1937 Manchester Corporation Transport's overhead gangs began a task which, at the time, must have seemed most unusual to them. Instead of dismantling the overhead equipment on abandoned tramway routes, they started preparing the span wires in some of the city's streets to take trolleybus wires. Soon the type of hanger already in use in London became a familiar sight in Ashton Old Road, down past London Road station, up Aytoun Street and Portland Street to the end of Piccadilly and along Newton Street, Great Ancoats Street, Swan Street, Rochdale Road to the new garage, and Thompson Street and Oldham Road back to New Cross. Slowly the pattern of twin wires was woven with all the necessary frogs and crossings and by late autumn all appeared to be approaching completion.

About the end of November a photograph of Crossley four-wheeler 1006 appeared in the local press and all seemed to be ready for the introduction of Manchester's trolleybuses. The inauguration of the new mode of transport did not take place for another three months, however, and the short three-window blue, white and red Ashton-under-Lyne balcony tramcars still shared the tracks in Parker Street and Piccadilly with the various types of Manchester car and Stockport's dainty four-wheelers. I remember that the old Ashton cars had become very noisy by that time and they all seemed to have one thing in common: a trolley pole with a distinct kink in it. During this period the trolley wires were kept apart from the tramway overhead even at intersections; the wires were taken over the top of the tram contact wires and treated as ordinary span wires with hangers and coupled up properly when they came into use.

I left the area at the end of 1937 but frequent visits thereafter kept me up to date. On one of these, about Easter 1938, I found the trolleybuses in service and the elaborate tramway track work at the junction of Fairfield Street and London Road replaced by straight track. There was a frequent service to Stalybridge on 28 and 29 to Ashton, with short workings on 29x to The Trough and Fairfield Road. The 26 tram service between Stevenson Square and Ashton via Ashton New Road, usually operated solely by Manchester's 'Pilcher' cars, had been discontinued and extra 26Bs were running as far as the Ashton 'frontier' at the Snipe. At that time there were no reversing facilities for trolleybuses at the

Snipe but trolleybuses could turn at Openshaw, near the junction with the 53 bus service, Fairfield and The Trough. The tram service beyond Fairfield to Guide Bridge had been replaced by the 15A (later 15x), Parker Street (Piccadilly) to Guide Bridge bus service in 1932. These journeys ran every 10 minutes, interleaving with the 30-minute services on the existing 15 bus, which ran through the city to Worsley and was joint with Salford.

My first ride, strangely enough, was on the prototype six-wheeler Crossley trolleybus that was Ashton 58 and already two years old, although I did not know it at the time. The bodywork on this vehicle resembled London Transport standards and contrasted with the streamlined design of the Manchester vehicles. Apart from brief encounters with the Hastings system and Ashton's earlier route to Hathershaw, I had no experience of trolleybuses and the Manchester and Ashton double-deckers were quite a novelty to me, being the first modern examples I had met. My main impression of the ride on 58 was that it was not as smooth as I had expected — the granite setts which formed the road would contribute to this — and it was not as fast nor had it the acceleration I had anticipated. I later found that the latter two criticisms were unjust as 58 had an 82hp motor, whereas the Manchester and subsequent Ashton vehicles had 85hp units

on the four-wheelers and 95hp on the six-wheelers. Ashton's use of trolley wheels was dictated by the ageing Hathershaw route and its old-fashioned overhead which was not suitable for skids. The Railless single-deckers that had worked the Hathershaw route for years were being withdrawn and the modern double-deckers had to take a turn on the route instead. My other recollections of that first sight of the system are that Manchester was mainly using six-wheelers but Ashton had both four and six-wheelers out, having at the time only four modern four-wheelers and three six-wheelers.

On my next visit in August 1938, the trams on the Ashton New Road had been withdrawn and 26s were running to Stalybridge, with 27s to Snipe and 27xs to Edge Lane, all worked by Manchester trolleybuses and starting from Stevenson Square. The first phase of the system was now complete and it was interesting that the six-wheelers still covered the principal workings.

On a visit in 1940 some of the new vehicles ordered in 1939 were in service — a photograph of 1144 had appeared in the trade press in April and four-wheelers were used in greater numbers on the regular services. Ashton, too, had had eight four-wheelers delivered, almost identical to the Manchester Crossleys. When the first Moston service started, in 1940, it ran via

Philip Groves' first trip on the trolleybus system was on the six-wheel Crossley prototype, Ashton 58, pictured here outside Ashton's garage in Mossley Road. Its service number indicator has been panelled over — Ashton used service numbers for a time and then, unusually, gave them up, showing only a destination on its buses, only to reintroduce them after the war.
Don Jones

Left: Leyland 1136 before delivery from English Electric, Preston. Its Princess Road garage blinds did not indicate moves for wider adoption of trolleybuses. The firm was also bodying a large batch of Daimler COG5 motor buses for Manchester, which were allocated to Princess Road, and 1136 has accidentally been fitted with the wrong blinds. The English Electric bodies differed in many small details from their Crossley counterparts.
English Electric via David Beilby

Below left: Crossley took newly-finished 1144 to Guide Bridge to be photographed outside the Odeon Cinema. Its corner bumpers are white-painted and it has the mandatory wartime lighting restrictions — only the nearside headlamp had a bulb, its beam masked with a steel shutter. 1136 would be similarly treated before entering service. Unlike the 1000-series, the 1100-series had clips for 'slip boards' beneath the front destination blind; on the trolleybuses these were rarely, if ever, used.
Crossley Motors/Ian Allan Library

Lower left and below: All the 1100-series had the deeper seats, panelled interior upper-deck roof and other improvements introduced some months before on the motor buses. Very comfortable they were, with red leather upstairs, red, grey and white patterned moquette with leather trim in the lower saloon and glossy varnished timber trim round the windows and roof panelling. These pictures show both decks of 1126. The Streamliners had two safety mirrors on the stairs, so that the guard could see the upper saloon or platform. In the lower saloon, above the (empty) fare table case, there is a small square varnished box marked *'Bus Guide. Not to be taken away'*; war restrictions meant that it was never filled. On the platform there are two messages from the safety and litter conscious Department: *'Warning, do not pass behind this bus until you KNOW the road is clear'* and *'Please deposit used tickets in this box'*.
English Electric via David Beilby

Swan Street on the outward journey from its temporary city terminus at Stevenson Square, and a new bay of wiring was erected there, on the south-west side of the square. The Ashton service then used the new bay and the Moston services used the bay in the centre of the square, which had previously been used by the 26.

spent some time in the area between November 1940 and August 1941 and on each visit I always looked for signs of the extension to Blackley. A double junction had been put in and about twenty yards of overhead but nothing more was done except that at busy times trolleybuses numbered 60x would run to and from Moston Lane along Rochdale Road, having to return via Conran Street as there were no turning facilities. The Blackley Estate route was never constructed.

When Hyde Road garage took over the Ashton Old Road workings in 1941, four-wheelers were to be found regularly on the Moston, Guide Bridge, Haughton Green services and many of the short workings on the Old and New Roads. The six-wheelers were confined to the Ashton and Stalybridge 26 and 28 services and would sometimes share the 30 with four-wheelers.

Manchester thus possessed a useful trolleybus system with very modern equipment. There was quite a difference in passenger comfort between the 1938 deliveries and those which came in 1940. The 1100-series vehicles had higher seat backs and deeper seat cushions and these two items, which had also been introduced on buses in 1939, gave a great improvement, although there was no discrimination in operation. The four-

wheelers of both years and both makes appeared on all the normal four-wheel duties. My personal favourites were the 1940 English Electric-bodied Leylands. These seemed to have a better finish than the Crossley bodies and gave a much smoother ride. All but three (1104, 1109 and 1133) spent all their lives at Rochdale Road garage and thus rarely appeared on the Greenheys, Haughton Green or Ashton Old Road services, which Hyde Road garage was working by this time.

During the first eight years or so there were various improvements to overhead which I noticed on successive visits. In Portland Street two bays were constructed to allow vehicles on different services to overtake and an extra line was put in so that in Oldham Street vehicles from Church Street used a separate wire from the Stevenson Square vehicles. Automatic turn-outs were installed at a few junctions and in one or two instances the turn-out was first set manually by the guard (Manchester's almost unique title for the conductor) and then reset automatically as the trolley skid passed under a resetting skate on the wire.

The trolleybus overhead in the city centre was originally insulated from that of the trams. Everywhere tramway and trolleybus

wiring intersected there was a long 'dead' section on the tramway contact wire and I recall vividly during one evening rush-hour seeing a tram which was proceeding out of Piccadilly into London Road stop under the trolleybus overhead leading out of Portland Street. There was some peering at cut-out switches and even a glance to see if the trolley had come off the wire before the crew gathered what had befallen them. No more time was wasted however, and a touch of the tram's trolley on the trolleybus positive wire soon gave the car sufficient momentum to reach its own 'live' wire again.

By the spring of 1941 I noticed that new section insulators had been installed on the tramway overhead in Market Street, just north of High Street, in Portland Street, Oldham Street, Lever Street and Newton Street, without feeders. The existing feeder in London Road remained unchanged as did that in Mosley Street, and the insulation between the trolleybus positive wire and the tramway wire was removed, so that for Piccadilly, Parker Street, Stevenson Square and the surrounding streets, trams and trolleybuses shared a common source of power. Even the negative trolleybus wire in this area was insulated from the rest of the system by section insulators in London Road, Aytoun Street and Newton Street.

Perhaps the most interesting vehicle development was the delivery to Ashton of six wartime Sunbeam trolleybuses, which looked strange amongst all the Manchester streamlining. With this increase the Ashton fleet numbered 21 units.

I have kept these recollections purposely to the early days of the system. I had always hoped that after the war there would be further expansion but apart from the Hyde service there was none. The older trolleybuses continued to operate, although the six-wheelers gradually disappeared from all-day service in favour of the four-wheelers.

Above and above right: During the war new buses were allocated by the government and Ashton received four Park Royal-bodied Sunbeams (61-64) in 1944, followed by two Roe-bodied examples (65-66) just after the war ended but still to utility specifications. 61 in Portland Street in February 1956 and 66 at the same location two years earlier. After the war extra wiring was added at the terminus to allow trolleybuses to overtake.
Ted Jones, Roy Marshall

Right: The huge traffic carried by the trolleybuses is shown in this May 1949 picture of the Portland Street rush-hour queue for the Ashton Old Road services. A fully-loaded Ashton Crossley pulls away from the stop and a Manchester six-wheeler is starting to load; there will be a line of four or five more behind it. Passing the two is a Crossley DD42 motor bus on service 106 to Hyde, soon to be converted to trolleybus 210.
MCT/Michael Eyre

The importance of the Moston services in saving fuel is shown by the timetable. The frequency varied little over the years; this is the 1948 edition.
Michael Eyre

TROLLEY BUS SERVICE No. 32.—MOSTON (Gardener's Arms) and MANCHESTER (Church Street) via Rochdale Road.
TROLLEY BUS SERVICE No. 33.—MOSTON (Ben Brierley) and MANCHESTER (Church Street) via Rochdale Road.

MONDAY TO SATURDAY.

		am	am	am			am	am	am	am	am	
Gardener's Arms	dep	...	5 27	...	and every	...	6 32	...	...	...	6 52	and every 7½ mins.
Ben Brierley	"	5 2	5 33	5 42	10 mins.	6 32	6 38	6 44	6 48	6 55	6 58 7 2	from Gardener'sA
Conran Street	"	5 5	5 36	5 45	from Ben	6 35	6 41	6 47	6 51	6 58 7 1	7 5	& every 4 mins.
Queen's Road	"	5 10	5 41	5 50	Brierley	6 40	6 46	6 52	6 56 7 3	7 6	7 10	from Ben Brierley
Church Street	arr	5 21	5 52	6 1	to	6 51	6 57	7 3	7 7	7 14	7 17 7 21	to

		am	am			am	am	am			pm	pm	pm	pm
Gardener's Arms	dep	...	9 15	and every	...	9 37	...	9 45	...	and at	...	1030	...	1034
Ben Brierley	"	9 17	9 21	7½ mins. from	9 40	9 43	9 47	9 51	9 54	similar	1032	1036	1039	1040
Conran Street	"	9 20	9 24	Gardener's	9 43	9 46	9 50	9 54	9 57	intervals	1035	1039	1042	1043
Queen's Road	"	9 25	9 29	Arms & B.B.	9 48	9 51	9 55	9 59	10 2	to	1040	1044	1047	1048
Church Street	arr	9 36	9 40	to	9 59	10 2	10 6	1010	1013		1051	1055	1058	1059

		am	am	am	am			am	am			am	am
Church Street	dep	5 22	5 42	5 54	6 2	and every	6 52	6 59	and approx. every	...	10 0	10 4
Queen's Road	"	5 33	5 53	5 6	6 13	10 mins.	7 3	7 10	7½ mins. to Gardener's	1011	1015
Conran Street	"	5 38	5 58	6 10	6 18	to Ben	7 8	7 15	Arms and every	1016	1020
Ben Brierley	"	5 41	6 1	6 13	6 21	Brierley	7 11	7 18	4 mins. to	1019	1023
Gardener's Arms	arr	...	6 19			to	...	7 24	Ben Brierley to	...	1029

		am	am	am	am			pm	pm			am	am
Church Street	dep	10 8	1012	1015		and at	1045	1049	11 0	11 0	...	...	...
Queen's Road	"	1019	1023	1026		similar	1056	11 0	1111	1111	...	...	...
Conran Street	"	1024	1028	1031		intervals	11 1	11 5	1116	1116	...	...	...
Ben Brierley	"	1027	1031	1034		to	11 4	11 8	1119	1119	...	...	...
Gardener's Arms	arr	...	1037				...	1114		1125	...	...	...

Increased Service at Rush Periods.

TROLLEY BUS SERVICE No. 34.—CONRAN STREET (Moston Lane) and MANCHESTER (Church St.)
MONDAY TO FRIDAY

From Conran Street to Church Street :
Dept. 6-38 a.m., 6-45 a.m., 7-8 a.m., 7-14 a.m., 7-22 a.m. and every 4 minutes to 9-2 a.m.
Dept. 5-22 p.m., 5-37 p.m. and 5-44 p.m.

From Church Street to Conran Street :
Dept. 6-56 a.m., 7-26 a.m., 7-32 a.m., 7-38 a.m., 7-42 a.m., 7-47 a.m. and every 4 minutes to 8-43 a.m.
Dept. 5-4 p.m., 5-19 p.m., 5-26 p.m., 5-33 p.m. and 6-1 p.m.

TROLLEY BUS SERVICE No. 36.—MOSTON (Gardener's Arms) and STEVENSON SQUARE (via Oldham Road).

MONDAY TO SATURDAY.

		am			am	am	am			pm	pm	pm	pm			
Gardener's Arms	dep	5 0	and		6 20	6 42	6 56	and		1033	1049	11 4	1126	...	...	...
Nuthurst Road	"	5 3	every		6 23	6 45	6 59	every		1036	1052	11 7	1129	...	...	...
Ben Brierley	"	5 6	20		6 26	6 48	7 2	7½		1039	1055	1110	1132	...	...	...
Queen's Road	"	5 16	mins.		6 36	6 58	7 12	mins.		1049	11 5	1120	1142	...	...	...
Stevenson Square	arr	5 25	to		6 45	7 7	7 21	to		1058	1114	1129	1151	...	...	...

		am			am	am	am			pm	pm					
Stevenson Square	dep	4 30	and		6 50	7 0	7 23	and		1045	11 0	...	...	...	...	...
Queen's Road	"	4 39	every		6 59	7 9	7 32	every		1054	11 9	...	...	...	...	...
Ben Brierley	"	4 49	20		7 9	7 19	7 42	7½		11 4	1119	...	...	...	...	...
Nuthurst Road	"	4 52	mins.		7 12	7 22	7 45	mins.		11 7	1122	...	...	...	...	...
Gardener's Arms	arr	4 55	to		7 15	7 25	7 48	to		1110	1125	...	...	...	...	...

SUNDAY.

		am	am	am			am	am	am	and		pm	pm	and		pm
Gardener's Arms	dep	6 0	6 30	7 0	7 30	8 0	8 22	and		3 22	3 35	and		1035
Nuthurst Road	"	6 3	6 33	7 3	7 33	8 3	8 25	every		3 25	3 38	every		1038
Ben Brierley	"	6 6	6 36	7 6	7 36	8 6	8 28	15		3 28	3 41	10		1041
Queen's Road	"	6 15	6 45	7 15	7 45	8 15	8 37	mins.		3 37	3 50	mins.		1050
Stevenson Square	arr	6 24	6 54	7 24	7 54	8 24	8 46	to		3 46	3 59	to		1059

		am	am	am	am	am	am			pm	pm					pm
Stevenson Square	dep	6 27	6 57	7 27	7 57	8 27	8 49	and		3 49	4 2	and		11 2
Queen's Road	"	6 36	7 6	7 36	8 6	8 36	8 58	every		3 58	4 11	every		1111
Ben Brierley	"	6 45	7 15	7 45	8 15	8 45	9 7	15		4 7	4 20	10		1120
Nuthurst Road	"	6 48	7 18	7 48	8 18	8 48	9 10	mins.		4 10	4 23	mins.		1123
Gardener's Arms	arr	6 51	7 21	7 51	8 21	8 51	9 13	to		4 13	4 26	to		1126

TROLLEY BUS SERVICE No. 37.—MOSTON (Ben Brierley) and STEVENSON SQUARE (via Oldham Road).

This Service operates at Rush Periods, Saturday Afternoons and Sundays to augment the 36 Service

Gallery — the Moston services

Collyhurst
1105 on Rochdale Road at Collyhurst Street in 1951 has an experimental six-line intermediate indicator blind. Although the terminus was in Church Street, for many years trolleybuses showed 'High Street' as the city destination. 'Church Street' was then added to newer blinds in the 1950s but (and confusingly to a stranger) buses would show either depending on the age of the blinds fitted. In the background are the long-demolished Collyhurst flats. Hilary Garments was one of many small firms in the city's 'rag trade'; its owner's 1949 Humber Hawk is parked outside.
Neville Knight/Chris Heaps

Queens Road
About half a mile further out, Queens Road crosses Rochdale Road. This April 1955 picture is of the city side of the junction, with 1109 inbound. Behind, on the 7x Queens Road to Crumpsall Hospital afternoon service, Leyland TD5 3396, turns into Scropton Street to go round the block, back to the stop for Crumpsall. Just by 3396 is trolleybus feeder and control box number 13. The window of 'Boots the Chemist' is well stocked but the next-door shop is empty.
Ray Dunning

Conran Street
The trolleybuses turned off Rochdale Road into the narrow Conran Street — the church spire at the corner can be seen in the previous picture. Leyland 1115 and Crossley 1168 pass at Carisbrook Street.
Ray Dunning

Moston Lane

'Moston Lane' terminus was at its junction with Upper Conran Street. Buses to the Ben Brierley and Gardener's Arms turned right; evening short-workings turned left to go back to Rochdale Road. Six-wheelers could not get round this corner and four-wheelers could not pass each other; the Department provided the large circular mirror to allow drivers to see if the road was clear. This March 1955 picture shows 1011 turning into Upper Conran Street, passing a Ford Consul. Dent's furniture store was offering television set rental at £1 deposit and £3-10s-0d weekly.
Chris Heaps

Hall Street

The 55 tram had terminated in Moston Lane at Hall (later Hillier) Street at the foot of Sankey's Brow, a few yards behind the trolleybus in this picture. The adjacent Terminus Inn kept its name long after the trams had gone. Beyond here to the Ben Brierley the Corporation had no legal powers to run trolleybuses, solving the problem with a wartime Emergency Order. The garage with the circular petrol sign in the background was owned by J. A. Ferrington, who started the 'Pioneer' bus service to Audenshaw that later became Mayne's. Leyland 1034 with a dented front panel on a sunny 24th April 1955.
Ray Dunning

Ben Brierley

Leyland 1109 has a faulty catch on its nearside windscreen and the driver has stuffed the joint with a copy of the *Manchester Evening News* to stop the draught. Behind 1109 is the Simpson Memorial with its library, meeting rooms and bowling green. The low building is Martin's Bank and by its side is the Museum Inn. Ben Brierley was a dialect poet and the pub that bears his name was across the road from the bank, on the corner of Kenyon Lane.
C. Carter/Ian Allan Library

Ben Brierley
Leyland 1111 in the terminal loop outside St Dunstan's Church. The bus will turn sharp back right to load for its 19-minute journey to town; the 212 is going to the Gardener's Arms and a coalman is delivering to one of the cottages on Moston Lane. Mid-1955.
Ray Dunning

Moston Cemetery
The Moston via Oldham Road tram had run a quarter of a mile beyond the Ben Brierley, terminating by the large St Joseph's Roman Catholic Cemetery, where this spacious but little-used shelter was provided. It was hereabouts that the 'modern' 1930s private housing started, construction being halted by the war. From here to the Gardener's Arms the Corporation had no legal powers to run trolleybuses and the section was also built under the wartime Emergency Order. Crossley 1027 on 14th April 1955.
Ray Dunning

Nuthurst Road
At Nuthurst Road there were extensive playing fields, part used for a Polish refugee camp during the war. Beyond was New Moston with the large modern Lightbowne council estate. Nuthurst Road turning circle was at the traffic island in the centre background. The tall chimney is that of Moston Mill, one of the newer cotton mills, constructed in 1910. 1020 draws away from the Nuthurst Road stop on 7th October 1954.
Ray Dunning

Gardener's Arms
On a quiet Sunday in October 1954, 1136 on service 211 turns at the roundabout at the junction of Moston Lane, Victoria Avenue, Greengate and Lightbowne Road. The 1943 extension to the A. V. Roe factory continues straight along Greengate.
Neville Knight

Gardener's Arms
On a busier day, 1133 is ready to depart for Stevenson Square, the side of the pub just in picture. A passenger hurries to catch the bus; had he missed it there would have been only a seven minute wait for the next 211 or three minutes if a 212 would do. Manchester Leyland PD2 3246 is on motor bus service 26, which went to the city via Charlestown Road, Blackley and Crumpsall — for some years this service number duplicated that of the Ashton New Road trolleybuses. Also in the picture is Oldham Corporation Crossley-bodied Daimler CVD6 326 on Oldham's service D to that town.
Ted Jones

BUT to Moston
BUT 1302 arrived some three months ahead of the rest, in time to do a few turns on the 211; this June 1955 picture is probably its first. It was the only BUT that worked to Moston, the 211 having been converted by the time the others were delivered.
Michael Eyre

Kenyon Lane
At the Ben Brierley, the Oldham Road service turned into Kenyon Lane. On a Sunday in June 1955 17-year-old 1034, its indicators nicely set, has just left the Ben; the pub is hidden behind the bus. The fish and chip shop on the corner of Penn Street has an appropriate advert for Saxa salt on its wall.
P. G. Mitchell

Newton Heath
On that same Sunday, 1117 turns from Thorp Road into Oldham Road. Behind the bus Thorp Road rises to cross the railway to Oldham and Yorkshire. The brick tower beyond is the part of the former Lancashire and Yorkshire Railway Carriage Works that the City Council caused the Transport Committee to investigate as a potential trolleybus garage.
P. G. Mitchell

Miles Platting
Much nearer the city centre, 1131 passes the Osborne Cinema in Miles Platting. Oldham Road was wide and, for some reason, the overhead running wires were placed close to the centre of the roadway, making it awkward for drivers to pull close to the kerb at some stops. The car, ANE 45, is a 1934 Triumph Gloria and the outbound bus is Manchester PD1 3045 on service 54 to Middleton.
Ray Dunning

Stevenson Square
This picture, taken in July 1954, looks west towards Oldham Street. In 1948, the Moston terminus had moved from the shelter by the inspector's hut to a new island off camera to the left of the photographer.
Ray Dunning

Stevenson Square
1108's crew pose for Ray Dunning to take their picture. A long-time member of the Queens Road garage platform staff, Ray took many of the pictures in this book. The guard has put his ticket machine box in the pavement in front of the 'keep left' bollard. The driver holds a brew can in which the crew would carry hot tea. The Department provided facilities for 'brewing up' at several termini but 1108 would not be late departing because operations were under an inspector's watchful eye. Inspector Dick Airey was on duty on 21st April 1955.
Ray Dunning, Ray Dunning

Six

Completion

In 1945 erection of overhead recommenced with the extension of service 30 from the University to Greenheys, passing the then home of Manchester City Football Club at Maine Road, shared at the time by Manchester United, whose ground at Old Trafford had been a further victim of the blitz. The service was extended as the overhead was completed as far as Moss Lane East on 14th January 1946, where there was a turn-back, and to Platt Lane on 20th February. A siding was provided on Lloyd Street South so that trolleybuses, especially the six-wheelers, could handle much of the Saturday football crowds. The 30 was finally completed on 12th July 1948 with the extension down Miller Street, then largely devoid of buildings due to the blitz, to Corporation Street.

The ending of the war allowed the revision of Manchester's comprehensive all-night bus, tram and trolleybus services in August 1946. To the Snipe there were separate 27x from Stevenson Square via Ashton New Road and 28x from Piccadilly via Ashton Old Road. A 32x all-night service from Church Street to Moston via Rochdale Road was also introduced. The 32x and 27x were altered to start in Piccadilly in 1947/8, coming into the city via Newton Street and going out by the unusual route of Newton Street and Stevenson Square.

The prolonged severe winter of 1946/47 resulted in acute shortages of coal — rail movements were paralysed and stocks at power stations ran out. Industry suffered major power cuts, some firms having to close down. Domestic supplies were severely restricted and the power cuts, low voltages and load shedding affected the trolleybus system, as did the weeks of ice and snow. Many services were reduced. In Ashton, for example, the voltage was so low that a limit of three had to be placed on the number of vehicles allowed into the Snipe to Ashton section; more than that and vehicles came to a halt. At rush hours trolleybuses queued at the Snipe waiting to enter the sector.

In spite of the wartime disruption and although the trolleybus system would be much larger than intended, the City Council remained determined to press ahead with the conversion of the Hyde tram service to trolleybuses — and in 1947 government permission was obtained to order the vehicles and overhead equipment. The route was long and straight with frequent stops and heavy traffic — eminently suitable for trolleybuses. It also passed Hyde Road garage.

The extension of service 30 from the University to Greenheys was completed in 1946 and the city section to Corporation Street two years later. This picture of BUT 1360 about to descend Miller Street to Corporation Street is particularly apposite because the whole of the area in front of the bus was flattened by the blitz. The tower of Strangeways prison is on the mid-horizon to the left of the bus; it would not have been visible in 1939. Although this picture was taken in 1959, the blitzed area remained undeveloped.
Peter Thompson

The plan was changed in one important detail. The short Reddish Lane section, from Hyde Road to the Bull's Head was deleted — there were plans for motor bus cross-city working into Salford. These came to fruition in 1951 with the introduction of the very busy joint Manchester / Salford services 57/77 from Swinton and Pendlebury to Reddish. There was, however, to be an extension in Hyde, where the trolleybuses were to run to Gee Cross, a mile or so beyond Hyde town centre and only a short distance from the boundary of the Borough of Stockport. Curiously, in the Department's fare tables and some traffic notices the Gee Cross terminus was referred to as 'Apethorn Lane' — a minor track off Dowson Road leading to a mill.

Crossley 1147 at the Corporation Street terminus close to the junction of Miller Street and Ducie Bridge. As usual for the trolleybuses this was at the edge of the city centre and slightly too far from Victoria Station to attract casual passengers.
Neville Knight

Contracts were placed with Crossley Motors for 38 four-wheelers (1200-1237) and 16 six-wheelers (1240-1255), all with Crossley bodies to Manchester's standard postwar design. The 10 extra vehicles were to cover SHMD's decision not to buy trolleybuses and the Gee Cross extension.

Road reconstruction in Hyde caused a premature end to tramcar operation beyond the Denton/Hyde boundary at Broomstair Bridge after 30th December 1947 and for a few months a shuttle service of SHMD buses connected with the Manchester trams. Construction of the

overhead by Manchester and SHMD staff in their respective areas was soon completed but the delivery position for new buses, diesel or electric, was acute with materials under government allocation, priority being given to motor buses. The Corporation's priorities were the same; construction of the new trolleybuses would have to wait.

Construction of Crossleys 1200-1237 was deferred until 1949 and even then was slow, delivery taking seven months. The six-wheelers did not arrive until 1951, their registration numbers, issued in 1948, looking very out of date. By this time AEC had acquired Crossley Motors and its marketing department gave the new trolleybuses model names — 'Empire' for the four-wheelers and, by some curiously inverted thinking, 'Dominion' for the massive-looking six-wheelers. The names did nothing to gain sales and, apart from two chassis for Cleethorpes, the Manchester and Ashton vehicles were unique.

Replacement of the trams could not wait. From 14th March 1948 tram service 19 was replaced by a motor bus service between Manchester and Hyde. Numbered 106, it operated until 15th January 1950, by which time sufficient new trolleybuses had been delivered. In the meantime the Corporation's last tramcar ran on 10th January, 1949.

Time for some more renumbering of services. The Hyde trolleybus service was originally to be numbered 24 — a number

Above: Greenheys terminus was at the edge of the 1930s council estate; 1225 turns from Hart Road into Platt Lane, crossing the disused tram track.
Neville Knight

Below: Operated by a separate set of crews who worked only at night, Manchester's all-night bus network was one of the most comprehensive in the country. This page from the 1946 leaflet details the three new trolleybus-operated services.
Michael Eyre

Below: Operational economies eventually caused the all-nights to be changed to motor bus operation but the Ashton Old and New Road services continued to be scheduled for trolleybus operation until mid-1964, although increasingly diesels were used. This picture, taken at 07.00hrs on Friday 15th March 1963, is of brand-new Leyland PD2 3672, which had worked the Ashton Old Road all-night service and returned to Hyde Road garage at around 5.40am. It was immediately commandeered by a night fitter responding to an emergency call to replace a punctured tyre on a trolleybus on the 210. Behind, 1320 has arrived with the first journey on the 212, the 6.15am from Audenshaw.
Ted Jones

that appeared on the Department's 1948 route map, in company with the 24 motor bus from Stevenson Square to Rochdale. Second thoughts prevailed and it was then scheduled to become the 36, which involved renumbering the Moston services again, the 36 and 37 becoming 31 and 31x — clashing with the motor buses to Bramhall. This change had not long been done when it proved unnecessary, for a new plan was devised to get rid of the duplicated service numbers by (eventually) moving all the trolleybus services into the 210-219 group. When it finally commenced in 1950 the Gee Cross service was therefore numbered 210. This was a considerable achievement even for Manchester — a service that was twice renumbered before it started.

The apparently odd choice of '21-' was determined by the physical size of Manchester's number indicators; '21' could be squeezed into the 'tens' blind of the time, whereas '20' could not. The other trolleybus services were renumbered — 27, 26, 17, 28, 29 becoming 215, 216, 217, 218, 219 but the others were not done with any urgency. Service 30 was renumbered 213 in 1952 and the Moston services were altered in 1953, 31, 31x, 32, 33 and 34 becoming 211, 211x, 212, 212x and 214.

The 210 service commenced on 16th January 1950, Crossleys 1220-1237, which had been in store for some months, were licensed for its opening. 1200-1219 had been put into service on delivery to allow older vehicles to be taken out of service for overhaul. All were allocated to Hyde Road.

The route was 8.9 miles long and, somewhat surprisingly, the police allowed it to use the same terminal point as had the 106 bus. This was in George Street, at the 'busy' end of Piccadilly and the opposite end of Piccadilly Gardens from the other trolleybuses, 210 buses running inwards along the full length of Piccadilly. It was only a small concession as the 19 tram had run the full length of Market Street to Victoria Street, near Exchange Station. The Hyde trolleybuses were originally to have joined the 28 and 29s in Portland Street.

The 210 left the city along Parker Street (like George Street, it was better known as part of Piccadilly Bus Station), Portland Street, passing the existing trolleybus terminus, turning right into Piccadilly (which becomes London Road at the foot of the station approach), Downing Street and Ardwick Green and then began the long straight run along Hyde Road. At Ardwick Green it crossed the Greenheys route at right angles, although there was no connection here until 1959 when a curve was installed from Higher Ardwick into Hyde Road to allow the Devonshire Street North, Higher Ardwick, Hyde Road loop to be used as a test run for vehicles which had been in the Car Works — the trams were

gone but the works' name remained.

To serve the busy Belle Vue Pleasure Gardens, Funfair and Zoo (all now long-gone) the plan was to wire a loop to the Department's lay-by in Mount Road and poles were erected for this. It was then decided that the traffic congestion caused by the right turn from Hyde Road would be too great and instead a turning circle was installed a hundred yards closer to the city at Gorton Baths. Further out, the Thornley Park turning circle came into its own during the Suez crisis, described in a later chapter, whilst modifications to the loop at Denton provided connections to the 217 in both directions. That this was the case was not immediately apparent and one had to walk around the side streets involved and look at the wiring to convince oneself that it was indeed so.

Leaving Denton the route dipped down the hill to Broomstair Bridge over the River Tame and into Cheshire and SHMD's operating area. SHMD's overhead wiring, whilst adequate, was not carried out to Manchester's standards and would become distinctly droopy in hot weather. Instead of using the part-finished loop in Hyde centre, a new turning loop for the Hyde short workings was installed about half a mile further on at Smithy Lane, serving more of the shops and mills in the town's centre. At Gee Cross there was a large turning circle at the junction with Dowson Road, notable for having no supporting central pole and for its resultant floppy wiring.

The 1951 timetable of the 210 was typical of many of Manchester's principal bus services of the time. Very different from the bus services of 2007, it illustrates how personal transport has developed to the detriment of public facilities. Between 04.23 and 05.23 five vehicles left Hyde Road for Smithy Lane, followed by one at 05.28 for Gee Cross. The first bus returned from Smithy Lane at 04.57 and ran to Piccadilly whence it worked the first city departure at 05.37. Thereafter buses ran every ten minutes, increasing to two buses every fifteen minutes at rush hours together with many extra rush-hour short workings. After the 22.10 departure from Gee Cross buses ran back to Hyde Road garage from the outer end of the service, the last three

Abandonment of the Hyde tram service could not wait until the new trolleybuses arrived. Tramcar 270 in Piccadilly on service 19 to Hyde in 1947 a few weeks before the service was converted to motor bus service 106 as a temporary measure. Although widely known for his buses, Stuart Pilcher had introduced new tramcars to the Manchester fleet. Officially named 'Pullmans', to his intense irritation they became known as 'Pilchers'. *OTA/R. W. A. Jones*

outward journeys going only as far as Smithy Lane, with the last bus arriving at Hyde Road at 00.11. This gave the 210 the longest working day of any of the Department's services, although that of several others was only a few minutes less. In the odd four hours when the trolleybuses were not abroad it was possible to travel the 210 route as far as Thornley Park on the 57x all-night bus service.

In 1959 schedules on the 210 were reduced and a fifteen minute service then applied up to 07.41, followed by a ten minute service, with extras, in the morning peak. There was then a twelve minute frequency until 13.45, ten minutes until 16.15 and two buses every fifteen minutes in the evening peak, reverting to a twelve minute service in the evening, with the last bus still at 23.00.

The vehicles associated with the service, always based at Hyde Road garage, were Crossleys 1200-1237 and 1240-1255. The prewar stock was never allocated to the main or rush-hour 210, appearing on it only on special occasions.

Union opposition increasingly curtailed the use of Manchester's six-wheelers and there was some justification in the case of 1240-1255, for all the new Crossleys had very heavy steering, exceptionally so on the six-wheelers. The Department's engineers soon solved the problem, caused by errors in the design geometry of the wheels and king pins resulting in very strong castor action, and it was then hoped that the six-wheelers could be used on all-day service on the 210. This was tried but after the first morning rush-hour they all returned to garage, the union refusing to work them on all-day weekday service.

The City Council remained determined to press on with the Hyde conversion and 54 new trolleybuses were ordered. It was hoped they would be available by late 1947 but government priority was for motor buses and it was 1949 before delivery started. Brand-new 1205 and 1204 in Portland Street in May 1949. The driver of 1205 is discussing something with the inspector and guard — it was probably his first encounter with the very heavy steering.
Crossley Motors via Omnibus Society Library/Ted Jones

Crossley 1204 is attracting the interest of passers by, although the dog seems unimpressed. 1204 has a Crossley maker's transfer on its front panels but 1205 does not — by this time Crossley Motors had been taken over by AEC which had decided to phase out the Crossley name and badge. AEC would not allow Crossley to buy new transfers but could not stop the staff using up the existing stocks.
Crossley Motors via Omnibus Society Library/Ted Jones

As might be expected, Ashton bought five more or less identical four-wheel Crossleys, numbered 77-81. This is number 79 when new in 1950. The roadway is paved with granite setts, the abandoned tram tracks having been covered with tarmac.
D. A. Thompson via Ted Jones

TROLLEY BUS SERVICE No. 210   PICCADILLY, DENTON, HYDE and GEE CROSS.
MONDAY TO FRIDAY.

		am	am	am	am	am	am	am	am	am	am	am	am	am	am	am	am	am
Piccadilly	dep	...	...	...	...	...	5 37	5 52	...	6 12	...	6 27	...	6 42	...	6 57	...	
Devonshire Street	,,	4 23	4 38	4 54	5 8	5 23	5 28	5 45	6 0	6 13	6 20	6 29	6 35	6 44	6 50	6 59	7 3	7 14
Belle Vue	,,	4 30	4 45	5 1	5 15	5 30	5 35	5 52	6 7	6 20	6 27	6 36	6 42	6 51	6 57	7 6	7 10	7 21
Denton	,,	4 42	4 59	5 15	5 29	5 44	5 49	6 6	6 21	6 34	6 41	6 50	6 56	7 5	7 11	7 20	7 24	7 35
Smithy Lane, Hyde	,,	4 51	5 9	5 25	5 39	5 54	5 59	6 16	6 31	6 44	6 51	7 0	7 6	7 15	7 21	7 30	7 34	7 45
Gee Cross	arr	...	...	...	...	...	6 5	6 22	6 37	6 50	6 57	7 6	7 12	7 21	7 27	7 36	7 40	7 51

		am	am	am	am	am	am	am	am		am	am	am		pm	pm	pm	pm
Piccadilly	dep	7 12	...	7 27	7 37	7 45	7 53	8 0			9 0	9 10	9 20		3 40	3 48	3 55	4 3
Devonshire Street	,,	7 20	7 29	7 35	7 45	7 53	8 1	8 8	every		9 8	9 18	9 28	every	3 48	3 56	4 3	4 11
Belle Vue	,,	7 27	7 36	7 42	7 52	8 0	8 8	8 15	7½		9 15	9 25	9 35	10	3 55	4 3	4 10	4 17
Denton	,,	7 41	7 50	7 56	8 6	8 14	8 22	8 29	mins.		9 29	9 39	9 49	mins.	4 9	4 17	4 24	4 31
Smithy Lane, Hyde	,,	7 51	8 0	8 6	8 16	8 24	8 32	8 39	to		9 39	9 49	9 59	to	4 19	4 27	4 34	4 41
Gee Cross	,,	7 57	8 6	8 12	8 22	8 30	8 38	8 45			9 45	9 55	10 5		4 25	4 33	4 40	4 47

			pm	pm	pm		pm	pm	pm	pm						
Piccadilly	dep		6 40	6 50	7 0		1030	1040	1050	A	11 0	...	...	...	...	...
Devonshire Street	,,	every	6 48	6 58	7 8	every	1038	1048	1058	11 0	11 8	...	...	...	...	...
Belle Vue	,,	7½	6 55	7 5	7 15	10	1045	1055	11 5	11 7	1115	...	...	...	...	...
Denton	,,	mins.	7 9	7 19	7 29	mins.	1059	11 9	1119	1121	1129	...	...	...	...	...
Smithy Lane, Hyde	,,	to	7 19	7 29	7 39	to	11 9	1119	1129	...	1139	...	...	...	...	...
Gee Cross	arr		7 25	7 35	7 45		1115	...	...	...	...	...	...	...	...	...

MONDAY TO FRIDAY.

		am	am	am	am	am	am	am	am	am	am	am		am	am	am	
Gee Cross	dep	...	...	...	...	...	6 7	6 22	6 37	6 52	7 0	7 8	7 15		9 30	9 40	9 50	every
Smithy Lane, Hyde	,,	4 52	5 12	5 27	5 42	5 57	6 13	6 28	6 43	6 58	7 6	7 14	7 21	every	9 36	9 46	9 56	10
Denton	,,	5 2	5 22	5 37	5 52	6 7	6 23	6 38	6 53	7 8	7 16	7 24	7 31	7½	9 46	9 56	10 6	mins.
Belle Vue	,,	5 16	5 36	5 51	6 6	6 21	6 37	6 52	7 7	7 22	7 30	7 38	7 45	mins.	10 0	1010	1020	to
Devonshire Street	,,	5 23	5 43	5 58	6 13	6 28	6 44	6 59	7 14	7 29	7 37	7 45	7 52	to	10 7	1017	1027	
Piccadilly	arr	5 31	5 51	6 6	6 21	6 36	6 52	7 7	7 22	7 37	7 45	7 53	8 0		1015	1025	1035	

		pm	pm	pm	pm		pm	pm	pm		pm	pm	pm	pm		pm	pm	pm
Gee Cross	dep	4 10	4 18	4 25	4 33		6 40	6 50	7 0		1010	1017	1027	1037		1117	...	...
Smithy Lane, Hyde	,,	4 16	4 24	4 31	4 39	every	6 46	6 56	7 6	every	1016	1023	1033	1043	every	1123	1130	1140
Denton	,,	4 26	4 34	4 41	4 49	7½	6 56	7 6	7 16	10	1026	1033	1043	1053	10	1133	1140	1150
Belle Vue	,,	4 40	4 48	4 55	5 3	mins.	7 10	7 20	7 30	mins.	1040	1047	1057	11 7	mins.	1147	1154	12 4
Devonshire Street	,,	4 47	4 55	5 2	5 10	to	7 17	7 27	7 37	to	1047	1054	11 4	1114	to	1154	12 1	1211
Piccadilly	arr	4 55	5 3	5 10	5 18		7 25	7 35	7 45		1055	A	...	...		...	...	...

A—To Ardwick Green

Trolleybus services, July 1950

30	**Corporation Street — Ancoats — Ardwick Green — University — Greenheys, Platt Lane**
31	**Stevenson Square — Oldham Road — Moston, Ben Brierley — Moston, Gardener's Arms**
31x	Stevenson Square — Oldham Road — Moston, Ben Brierley
32	**Church Street — Rochdale Road — Moston, Ben Brierley — Moston, Gardener's Arms**
33	**Church Street — Rochdale Road — Moston, Ben Brierley**
33x	Church Street — Rochdale Road — Moston Lane (pm)
34	Church Street — Rochdale Road — Moston Lane (am)
210	**Piccadilly — Hyde Road — Denton — Hyde — Gee Cross**
210x	Piccadilly — Hyde Road — Denton — Hyde
210x	Piccadilly — Hyde Road — Denton
215	**Stevenson Square — Ashton New Road — Audenshaw, Snipe**
215x	**Stevenson Square — Ashton New Road — Droylsden, Edge Lane**
215x	Stevenson Square — Ashton New Road — Clayton, North Road
216	**Stevenson Square — Ashton New Road — Audenshaw — Ashton — Stalybridge**
216x	Stevenson Square — Ashton New Road — Audenshaw — Ashton
217	**Ashton — Guide Bridge — Denton — Haughton Green**
217x	Ashton — Guide Bridge — Denton
217x	Ashton — Guide Bridge
218	**Piccadilly — Ashton Old Road — Audenshaw — Ashton — Stalybridge**
218x	Piccadilly — Ashton Old Road — Audenshaw — Ashton
218x	**Piccadilly — Ashton Old Road — Audenshaw, Snipe**
219	**Piccadilly — Ashton Old Road — Guide Bridge — Ashton**
219x	Piccadilly — Ashton Old Road — Guide Bridge
219x	Piccadilly — Ashton Old Road — Audenshaw Road, The Trough
219x	Piccadilly — Ashton Old Road — Higher Openshaw, Fairfield Road
219x	Piccadilly — Ashton Old Road — Openshaw, Grey Mare Lane

Services shown in light type were rush-hour or part day

MANCHESTER CORPORATION TRANSPORT DEPARTMENT.

CORPORATION STREET AND GREEHEYS (Platt Lane)
SERVICE NO. 30.

COMMENCING ON MONDAY, 21st. APRIL 1952, THE ABOVE
SERVICE WILL BE RE-NUMBERED 213.

A. F. NEAL,
General Manager.

31st. MARCH 1952.

SHMD was responsible for the overhead beyond Broomstair Bridge and its overhead wiring could best be described as adequate. In this October 1949 picture, taken at Broomstair Bridge during an inspection before the service started, 1227's driver and a Manchester inspector look concerned. SHMD's tower wagon, converted from Thornycroft LC single-deck bus 118 (LG 3043), is in attendance.
Metropolitan Vickers via David Beilby

It is a popular myth that the postwar Crossleys never worked on the Ashton New Road services. In fact, they often did so after Rochdale Road closed to trolleybuses. 1208 in Stevenson Square on 18th March 1959.
J. S. Cockshott Archive

Gallery — The Hyde service

Piccadilly
The city terminus of the 210 was in George Street, at the opposite end of Piccadilly Gardens to the Ashton Old Road services. This brought the trolleybuses closer to the city centre but was only a minor concession by the police, as the Hyde trams had run down Market Street to Victoria Street and Deansgate. 1202 in new condition on a summer Sunday in 1952. The city is quiet but there was still a bus on the 210 every 7 or 8 minutes.
OTA/Harry Luff

Thornley Park
The first turn-back on the 210 was at Gorton Baths for Belle Vue; the next was at Thornley Park where Crossley Motors' photographer took this March 1951 picture of six-wheeler 1249. Behind the front of the bus, down Laburnum Road, is a Salford Daimler on the joint Manchester and Salford cross-city 57 service to Swinton which had commenced in January. The 1200-series had slip board brackets below their indicators but those on the six-wheelers were removed before delivery.
Crossley Motors

Denton
At Denton, 210x short-working trolleybuses turned right into Stockport Road towards Haughton Green and then left round a loop of side streets to return to Manchester. 1240 turns from Stockport Road into Inman Street in June 1959. In the background is Crown Point and beyond is the chimney of the works of battery maker Oldham and Son Ltd (advertising catchphrase: *'I told 'em Oldham'*), at the time the largest employer in Denton.
Peter Caunt

Broomstair Bridge
At Broomstair Bridge the River Tame is the boundary between the towns of Denton and Hyde, the counties of Lancashire and Cheshire, and Manchester Corporation and SHMD overhead wiring. Each authority supplied one of the poles at the break. On the right is a green-painted Manchester one, its cast iron base and pointed finial showing that it dates from the tramways; on the left is a plain silver-grey-painted SHMD. White bands on the poles mark a break between two power supply sections and were an indication to drivers not to draw current whilst crossing the gap, to avoid arcing. 1225 inbound to Manchester with the 3.16pm journey from Gee Cross on Sunday 5th August 1962.
Peter Thompson

Hyde Market Place
The stalls of Hyde Market were left permanently in place but were deserted on Sunday 8th April 1962. At the traffic lights, the main A57 road to Glossop turns off towards the right of the picture. 1223 outbound for Gee Cross.
Peter Thompson

Smithy Lane
The turn-back for Hyde was a quarter-mile further up busy Market Street at Smithy Lane, where there was a convenient triangle of roads: left into Smithy Lane (beneath the chimneys in the picture) and right into Lumn Road to come back to Market Street. 1225 outbound for Gee Cross on Sunday, 8th April 1962.
Peter Thompson

Gee Cross
Gee Cross terminus was only a few yards from the Stockport Borough boundary at Pole Bank. Trolleybuses turned in a circle across the main Dowson Road to return to Stockport Road. The turning circle was large but had no central support pole and its wiring was prone to oscillations that could cause dewirement. Just before the turning circle, on a miserably wet October 1949 day during an inspection trip before the 210 service commenced, 1227 poses for Crossley's photographer. In the second picture, taken in August 1962, 1204's driver carefully negotiates the floppy wiring. The terminus was often referred to by Manchester as 'Apethorn Lane', the small side road from which the Humber is emerging.
Crossley Motors, Peter Thompson

All the services were operating in 1952; the total route length was 44 miles, of which 17 were outside the city boundary. Although the fleet had reached its peak total of 207 vehicles owned, the maximum total of operational vehicles was only 189. The new Crossley Dominion six-wheelers had effectively replaced eighteen of the prewar six-wheelers (five Crossleys and thirteen Leylands) which had been withdrawn by the time the last two Dominions entered service in October 1951. A month later, the total dropped to 187 when prewar four-wheelers 1033/35 were withdrawn. Trolleybuses were still a sensitive issue in the city and the withdrawn vehicles were stored under cover for two years or more, pending a decision whether to overhaul them or not. The first were sold in 1953 but some were retained until 1955.

The increasing costs of bus operation and a decline in passenger numbers prompted Albert Neal, who had succeeded Stuart Pilcher as General Manager in 1946, to consider the future of the trolleybus system in 1952. The report summarised the merits of different vehicles:

'Advantages of the Trolleybus
Electrical energy is cheaper than fuel oil and is home produced.
Longer vehicle life and lower vehicle maintenance costs.
Three-axle vehicles available, giving more seats.
More rapid acceleration, smoother silent running and no exhaust fumes.
Advantages of the Motorbus
Complete mobility and availability for all services.
Higher overall speeds on some types of service.
Cheaper vehicle and no outlay for overhead equipment.
Less traffic congestion, as vehicles are able to pass each other.
No dislocation of services due to current failure or damage to wires.
Does not incur rates.
No unsightly overhead lines, less difficult to operate in ice and snow
Breakdown confined to vehicle concerned............'

The apparently strange statement regarding rates is explained by a quirk of the law — a trolleybus system pays rates upon its overhead wiring and associated equipment, in the same way as businesses today pay rates on their premises. Item 7 also warrants explanation: in severe freezing conditions ice formed on the overhead wiring and empty trolleybuses would have to be run through the night to keep the wires free of it.

Albert Neal emphasised that cross-city services, which produced more revenue than those terminating in the city centre, would be limited. There was also much housing development on new estates at the outskirts of the city; services to these required at most a fifteen minute frequency which would not generate enough revenue

to cover the extra cost of overhead wiring.

He then reviewed the relative costs of energy — the Department and many other operators were waging a campaign against the recently imposed penal level of tax on diesel fuel. The cost of fuel oil was 1.573d per bus mile to which was added fuel tax of 3.432d per bus mile. Taking into account a proposed 11% increase, the price of electricity supplied at cost was 2.653d per bus mile which gave a saving of 2.352d per bus mile in favour of trolleybuses. Apart from this the motorbus had an advantage of 1.113d per bus mile in other operating costs, which reduced the trolleybus's advantage to 1.239d per bus mile. Thus it was the penal taxation of fuel oil that made it economic to operate fundamentally more expensive trolleybuses.

Wisely he pre-empted any possible resurgence of the Coal Lobby. *'For the power consumed by the six million vehicle miles per year covered by the trolleybuses the coal needed in a modern generating plant was about 10,700 tons; the fuel oil for the same number of bus miles was 666,000 gallons, which would cost the country £27,000 in imports. Whereas if the coal was exported and not used for power generation it could be sold abroad for £59,000.'* Thus it was more economic for the country to buy oil and sell coal, although this was hardly relevant to Manchester's finances.

He considered that only about one third of the Manchester bus network would be suitable for trolleybuses, specifically mentioning services:

25	Newton Heath — Greenheys
41/42	Royal Exchange — Chorlton/Didsbury
53	Trafford Park — Cheetham Hill
57/77	Swinton — Reddish
62	Heaton Park — Chorlton
65	New Moston — Trafford Park
75	Heaton Park — Greenheys
76	Brookdale Park — Greenheys
80	Piccadilly — Chorlton
81	Hightown — Chorlton
82	Hollinwood — Chorlton
109	Reddish — Victoria Station

In retrospect this list was hardly serious; the General Manager was making the point that services which generated sufficient revenue to pay for trolleybuses and their overhead wiring were the busy ones on

In 1952 the Department considered the future of its trolleybuses and whether their use should be extended. Services that would generate sufficient revenue to pay for the overhead wiring were the busy cross-city ones, conversion of which would have brought large numbers of trolleybuses onto the main city centre streets, to which the police would never agree. A police Rover and a police motorcycle squeeze past the turning Wolseley, nicely emphasising the reasons for the constabulary's continued opposition.
Manchester Libraries

which operation would be problematical. On the 'bus-a-minute' service 53, vehicles were constantly overtaking each other at stops; its operation with trolleybuses was barely sensible. The cross-city 25, 57/77, 62, 65, 75, 76, 81 and 82, and the 41/42 which worked a loop in the city centre, would all have brought large numbers of trolleybuses onto the streets that were the subject of police objections. What Salford's enterprising General Manager, Charles Baroth, thought of the 57/77 suggestion is probably unprintable.

However, anything concerning trolleybuses in Manchester had to be handled with care and the City Council had to be allowed to have its say. Diplomatically Albert Neal recommended that:

'(a) consideration of extension of the trolleybus system be deferred until the next programme of motor-bus replacement was completed
(b) sixty two new trolleybuses be purchased to maintain the existing services.
(c) representations be made to the Ministry of Transport and the Chancellor of the Exchequer to point out the economic position facing the department'.

The Council approved the report on 29th April 1953. Existing services would be retained but (and more significantly) no further extensions would be made to the system.

The approach to the Ministry brought a response which could have come straight from the scriptwriters of the satirical TV series 'Yes Minister': 'You will no doubt have seen that the Chancellor of the Exchequer made no reference to hydrocarbon oils in the recent budget and it is regretted that there is nothing further that this Ministry can do in this matter...'

Tenders were invited for the new vehicles.

The trolleybus had many merits but could be affected by events beyond an operator's control. On 12th June 1954, a serious fracture of a large water main near Lumn Road, Hyde, closed the road, requiring a route diversion. Trolleybuses continued to operate to Denton but for the service to Hyde the Department suddenly had to muster some 20 motor buses, even though the problem was not of its making. 1240 on the Denton short working and Leyland PD1 3184 on the main service.
Chris Heaps

In 1953 orders were placed for 62 new trolleybuses to replace the 1000-series. The BUT chassis were assembled at AEC's Crossley Motors, Errwood Park, works in Heaton Chapel. H. V. Burlingham Ltd of Blackpool built the bodies and took pictures of the last of the batch, 1362.
H. V. Burlingham Ltd

Before placing the order, Manchester asked Ashton and SHMD for their views. Ashton replied that it particularly wanted to retain its trolleybuses for at least ten years and, thus reassured, Manchester went ahead. Five years later Ashton was to urge trolleybus abandonment and receive scant sympathy for its change of heart.

Contracts were placed in October 1953 for 62 chassis from British United Traction Ltd ('BUT' — a joint AEC-Leyland company) with bodies by H. V. Burlingham Ltd of Blackpool and electrical equipment from Metropolitan Vickers (AEI Ltd) which was still based in Trafford Park. Numbered 1301-1362, their registration numbers, ONE 701-762, almost totally matched their fleet numbers — the Department was slightly too late asking the motor tax office to achieve this and in Albert Neal's Manchester it would have been unthinkable to number them 1701-1762 to match.

The first, 1302, was delivered on time and entered service in time to work on the surviving 211 service in Moston but the rest were delayed for months by problems at (by then ACV-owned) Crossley's Errwood Park, Heaton Chapel, works, where the chassis were assembled. This caused considerable difficulties for Burlingham, which had quoted on the basis it would build them in the months when its seasonal coach building was at a low, and for the Transport Department which had to keep fifty elderly about-to-be-withdrawn four-wheelers running for an extra six months.

Ashton, too, bought new vehicles — eight BUTs with bodies by S. H. Bond Ltd, a long-established, high-quality coachbuilder which had recently moved to a new works in Sharston, Wythenshawe and was making a determined effort to enter the bus-building market.

Before Manchester's BUTs arrived, however, the system's future had become clear — abandonment had started.

In 1955 and 1954 respectively, Ashton's wartime Sunbeams 63 and 64 were fitted with new bodies by Wythenshawe-based coachbuilder S. H. Bond Ltd. Number 64 arrived in a bright new livery of peacock blue and primrose, with a red band above the lower-deck windows. The blue and primrose were adopted but the red stripe did not meet with approval and was removed before 64 entered service.
OTA/Reg Wilson

In 1956 Ashton bought eight new BUTs, 82-89, also with well-designed Bond bodies. Numbers 88 and 85 in Portland Street on 12th July 1958.
J. S. Cockshott Archive

Bond's attempt on the bus market was progressing well but became beset by union demarcation disputes. Frustrated, the firm gave up the attempt and Ashton turned to another high-quality coachbuilder, Leeds-based C. H. Roe, which built new bodies on wartime Sunbeams 61/62 in 1958. As with 63/64 the work also involved fitting traction batteries and low voltage lighting but, unlike 63 and 64, the trolley base was not moved one bay forward. This picture is of 61.
Ted Jones

Although the City Council had agreed to maintain the existing network, it was somehow not surprising that in September 1954 there was a proposal to replace the Moston services. In his usual report Albert Neal referred to the April 1953 statement of future policy, in which it was indicated the 1100-series would require replacement with 69 new vehicles. Furthermore, during the next three or four years it would be necessary to renew the overhead on the Moston services. He recommended conversion to motor buses; 46 trolleybuses would be withdrawn.

The prewar trolleybuses were in less good condition than the motor buses of similar age. This came about through another anomaly in vehicle law. Motor-buses were subject to a Certificate of Fitness test and although this had been suspended during the war it was swiftly reimposed when it ended. The rules for trolleybuses were different, being defined, of all things, by the Railway Regulations, which required no such Certificate. Although Manchester's normal overhaul practice was the same for both types, after the war most of the capacity of the Car Works and that of its outside contractors had had to be concentrated upon overhauling the motor buses.

The result was that 1100-1176 ran for ten years or more before overhaul, as had several from the 1000-series. Both batches of four-wheelers had been in continuous all-day service for the whole of that period on some of the city's most heavily trafficked services and, whilst this was a tribute to Crossley, Leyland, Metropolitan-Cammell, English Electric and the staff at the garages, one tenth of the trolleybus fleet was now out of service as a result. Indeed such was the shortage of trolleybuses, due to failures and shortage of works staff, that some of 1100-1176 had not been overhauled by 1953.

In particular, the 1000-class, awaiting replacement, was in poor condition. For example, 1033 and 1035 had not run for two years because of water leaks in the upper deck. One of the authors particularly recalls the pools of water that swept back

and forth like a miniature tidal wave along the edges of the upper deck as the bus started and stopped, often cascading down the stairs — there was no electrical risk but it was unpleasant and certainly not what the Department wished. The bodies on six-wheelers 1059, 1071, 1072, 1077, 1081 were in such poor condition that they could not be used. Six otherwise serviceable trolleybuses were also off the road — 1104, 1133 and 1176 were finally being overhauled and 1146, 1167 and 1206 were awaiting spares from Crossley's new owner, AEC. In respect of 1206 this was a case of being slightly economical with the truth, as the replacement parts were needed as a result of severe accident damage. Nevertheless it took six months to get them.

At a cost of only £6,500 (£0.2 million) Rochdale Road garage could be converted for motor bus operation and extra bays wired at Hyde Road for the trolleybuses. Almost inevitably, these proposals were referred back by the City Council, which wanted more information. They were accepted at its next meeting in

October 1954.

In the intervening period the Moston residents suffered from a decaying system. Trolley poles showed signs of advanced age and had to be temporarily braced to adjacent ones or fitted with steel splints. The delay in delivery of the new BUTs meant that the 1000-series had to soldier on beyond their scheduled life and keeping them in service became difficult — complete seats missing from the upper deck, yet more floors awash with rainwater and frequent failures come to mind. The delay caused even more grief for the long-suffering Mostonians when 1302 appeared on the 211 service. Having for years been subjected to elderly vehicles which were draughty and leaky (the 1200-class was based at Hyde Road garage and never came to Moston), they were somewhat indignant at the appearance of the splendid 1302 just as the Oldham Road service was about to be converted, particularly as the

1302 at the Gardener's Arms on one of its few trips on the 211. The two intending lady passengers stare, as if unsure whether they can board the splendid new bus. *Ray Dunning*

When the first of the next new Leyland PD2s (3411-3470) were delivered, half the batch was allocated to Rochdale Road for the Moston services. Brand new 3436 turns at the Gardener's Arms in April 1956. *OTA/Reg Wilson*

replacement motor-buses allocated to Rochdale Road garage were hardly the cream of Manchester's fleet. Tactfully, 1302 was deployed elsewhere and, as soon as it was able, the Department did right by its customers — when the first of the next new Leyland PD2s (3411-3470) were delivered, half the batch was allocated to Rochdale Road for the Moston services.

By an unfortunate coincidence totally unconnected with the trolleybuses, the electricity supply in the Moston area had suffered several major breakdowns. These left the trolleybuses stranded and a varied collection of motorbuses would be fetched from all over the Manchester system to deputise. It was a tribute to the Department that it could organise this with an initial delay of only a few minutes and at first it was also wonderful for the enthusiast as old vehicles that had lurked unused in the back of garages joined brand new ones standing in for the marooned trolleybuses. However, the experience soon palled and even an enthusiast, queuing in the rain with the other Mostonians, began to wish an end to all trolleybuses.

Motor buses appeared on more and more of the peak hour journeys, partially to solve the vehicle shortage and also to get trolleybus staff accustomed to handling motor buses. The last Moston via Rochdale Road trolleybuses ran on Sunday 24th April 1955. Next day Leyland PD1s and PD2s from Rochdale Road garage and Daimler CVG6s from Princess Road garage worked a most useful new cross-city service, the first on Rochdale Road since the express services were split in 1932. Numbered 112/113 it absorbed the 49 (Piccadilly- Sale Moor) bus and operated Gardener's Arms — Piccadilly — All Saints — Sale Moor, with all-day short workings from Church Street to the Ben Brierley, numbered 114, and rush-hour shorts to the Conran Street loop as 114x.

Little of the overhead was removed until the 211 service was converted on 7th August 1955, the last journey from Gardener's Arms to Stevenson Square watched by a handful of enthusiasts. The replacement was simply the cross-city service that had been split in 1940 and it took up the old service number. The 80 ran from Hardy

Above left and above: To work its share of the new cross-city 112/113 to Sale Moor, Rochdale Road garage received six Leyland PD2s (3200-3202 and 3265-3267) from a reluctant Queens Road. This is Leyland-bodied 3265, new 1951, at the Gardener's Arms in April 1955. The Oldham Road service simply reverted to its prewar cross-city route to Chorlton, including the same service number, 80. For this Rochdale Road got some rather older Crossleys — 2133 at the Gardener's Arms in August 1955.
Ray Dunning

In the months before the conversion of the 211, many rush-hour journeys were diesel-worked in order to get drivers accustomed to motor buses, as here with Leyland-bodied Leyland TD5 3892 at the Gardener's Arms on 22nd April 1955. Most prewar Manchester buses did not have '21' on their indicator blinds but this crew had a good memory and have cleverly set the blinds to 31x, the previous service number.
Ray Dunning

A year after the Oldham Road conversion, the remaining trolleybuses were moved to Hyde Road garage, Rochdale Road becoming solely motor bus. During the period leading up to this, Rochdale Road would often turn out motor buses to work its rush-hour turns on the New and Old Roads. Leyland TD5 3376 leaves Rochdale Road garage for a turn on the 219x to Fairfield Road in April 1955.
Ray Dunning

Lane, Chorlton, to the Gardener's Arms, with short workings from Stevenson Square to Moston as 80x. It was during the last days of the 211 that the residents of Moston were treated to those few journeys on 1302. Over the next 12 months a phased reorganisation of services and garage allocations allowed Rochdale Road's trolleybuses to be progressively moved to Hyde Road, the final ones leaving on the night of 22/23 April 1956, one year after the 212 was converted.

Dismantling the Moston overhead lasted well into 1956. In the city centre, the wiring in Shudehill, Nicholas Croft, High Street, Church Street, and the Rochdale Road service wiring in Oldham and Swan Streets was also removed. The wires for the 213 in Swan Street (a parallel line to the Moston wiring), Rochdale Road, Thompson Street and Oldham Road remained, together with a spur to the power feeder at Rochdale Road garage. The fleet then numbered 143 with maximum service requirements of 138 (28 for the 210 service, 14 for the 213, 23 for the 215, 19 for the 216, 9 for the 217, 17 for the 218 and 28 for the 219).

The Anglo-French military action in Suez brought back restrictions on fuel oil and once again the trolleybuses were called upon. On 17th December 1956 the trunk 57/77 Reddish — Swinton service jointly operated by Manchester and Salford was temporarily split at Piccadilly in off-peak hours, the Piccadilly — Reddish section covered by trolleybuses on 210x, turning at Thornley Park. The Belle Vue short workings and the all-night 57x bus were also converted to trolleybus operation, again as 210x. On Saturdays the majority of the Maine Road football ground traffic was covered by trolleybuses on 213, and journeys from Audenshaw and Edge Lane to Maine Road were worked also by trolleybus. Such workings to Maine Road had once been a regular feature of Saturdays, from Moston too; with the ending of the Moston services, motor buses had taken over. Six-wheelers 1240-1255 saw full weekday service. The crisis passed; normal operations resumed on 1st April 1957.

Coincidentally also on 17th December 1956, as part of the new Piccadilly gyratory traffic scheme and the rebuilding of Piccadilly Bus Station, the terminus of the 210 service was moved from George Street to Portland Street, opposite the 218 and 219, with new wiring for trolleybuses to enter via London Road and leave via Aytoun Street. The 218 and 219 were similarly changed on 16th June 1957.

Police concern about traffic congestion prompted other changes. To avoid waiting trolleybuses blocking the gyratory system during rush hours, a siding was installed around the corner in Aytoun Street for peak

Above and below: The Suez crisis in the Middle East led to fuel rationing and from December 1956 to April 1957 the trunk cross-city 57/77 Swinton/Pendlebury — Reddish service was divided at Piccadilly during the day, the section to Reddish replaced by extra trolleybuses on 210x to Thornley Park. For the first time six-wheelers 1240-1255 saw all-day Monday-Friday service. Manchester 1200 at Thornley Park and Salford Daimler CVG6 383 in Piccadilly, February 1957.
Michael Eyre

Below: The gyratory traffic scheme in Piccadilly and the rebuilding of Parker Street Bus Station (after which its name was formally changed to Piccadilly Bus Station, which Mancunians had called it for 25 years) caused revision of the city termini and routes of the 210, 218 and 219. Trolleybuses came in up London Road to a new terminus across Portland Street from the old 218/219 stop, and left the city along Aytoun Street. 1249 and a four-wheeler at the new 210 terminus, 22nd April 1958.
J. S. Cockshott Archive

On the new inward route, 1304 passes the Fire Station on the left and Piccadilly station approach on the right. The tall building under construction is the 18-storey Rodwell Tower. Built over the Rochdale Canal, it has a working canal lock in its basement. The road sign for Ashton seems to be pointing in the wrong direction but right turns were banned to traffic coming along London Road from Ardwick and the sign directs drivers round the loop of Whitworth Street and Fairfield Street. A poster on the Store Street underbridge points to Volmax, pioneer of cut-price motor spares, located on Great Ancoats Street.
Peter Thompson

To avoid trolleybuses at the new Portland Street terminus blocking the gyratory system at peak times, a siding was installed around the corner in Aytoun Street for rush-hour journeys, some of which were renumbered 212. Ten years on, on 10th June 1965, 1350 is passed at the Aytoun Street terminus by Bolton Leyland Atlantean 217 working the 210, on loan at the request of new general manager Ralph Bennett. Previously at Bolton, where he had made considerable improvements to the appearance of the fleet, he would do the same at Manchester and 217's brief visit was the first step in major changes to Manchester's buses.
Peter Thompson

hour short workings on 218x and 219x, which were renumbered 212 and 212x. Some peak hour inwards and outwards 210x, 212, 212x and 219x continued to terminate by the Fire Station in Whitworth Street, well short of Piccadilly, showing 'London Road' as the inwards destination. To ease traffic flow at the busy Fairfield Street/London Road junction, the 210 left the city via Aytoun Street, Whitworth Street and London Road, whereas the 218 and 219 used Fairfield Street.

The next reduction in trolleybus services passed unnoticed by everyone. During 1957, the Department reached an agreement with A. Mayne & Son Ltd that the latter's local service from the Edge Lane trolleybus terminus, along Manor Road and Chappell Road to Sunnyside Road, would be extended to Stevenson Square. Commencing on 27th January 1958 and much welcomed by the local residents, limited stop motor bus service 46 was jointly operated by Mayne and the corporation. This was almost as much of milestone in the city's transport history as had been the introduction of trolleybuses but what went unnoticed was that it replaced half of the regular weekday 215x trolleybus service to Edge Lane, which was reduced from a 10 to a 20 minute frequency.

An extensive new gyratory traffic system at the junction of Droylsden Road and Manchester Road, Audenshaw, caused the Snipe terminus to be moved a few hundred yards closer to the city in May 1959, buses taking standing time outside the District Council's offices at Ryecroft Hall. Ashton Moss (Snipe) Colliery closed in that year. A new bus station was opened in Stalybridge and trolleybuses used it from 26th November 1959, involving reversing the direction of running round the Market Street and Waterloo Road loop. These changes were not an indication of faith in the trolleybus for with the benefit of hindsight it was already clear that the trolleybuses were to be abandoned and although the Department went through the formal steps of reviewing each case, there was never any real doubt about the outcome.

In 1959 the Co-operative Wholesale Society received permission to build a multi-storey office block at the corner of Miller Street and Corporation Street for the Co-operative Insurance Society. The city's first 'skyscraper' block and then one of the tallest buildings in Europe, it obliterated the terminus of the 213 and its construction provided a reason to convert the service to motor buses. The usual report was produced. It offered two obviously unpalatable trolleybus alternatives — extension across Ducie Bridge, which crosses the eastern end of Victoria Station, to a new turning point at New Bridge Street, or diversion of the trolleybuses down Shudehill and Withy Grove to Corporation Street rejoining the original route at the bottom of Miller Street. Both were speedily dismissed. The first was pointless as few passengers would wish to travel across the railway bridge. The police would not accept the reinstatement of trolleybuses through what was at the time the congested wholesale food market area of Shudehill and an extension down Withy Grove, with its busy newspaper offices and printing presses, let alone risk dewirements at its busy junction with Corporation Street. The recommendation was to convert to buses and use the Withy Grove route. Everyone agreed.

Above right: In 1957 the Department finally came to an agreement with A. Mayne & Son Ltd, whereby Mayne's local service from Sunnyside Road, Droylsden, to the trolleybus terminus at Edge Lane was extended to Stevenson Square, replacing half the 215x trolleybus service. Jointly-operated by Mayne and the Corporation, it was numbered 46 and started on 27th January 1958. Arthur Mayne supplemented his purchases of new AECs with judiciously selected second-hand units, including two former Leeds Corporation 1935 AEC Regents with 1946 Roe bodies. AUM 407 is about to leave the Stevenson Square terminus of the 46 on 29th April 1959 with a full load.
J. S. Cockshott Archive

Right: In Audenshaw, a new gyratory system was built at the junction of Droylsden Road and Manchester Road, a few hundred yards before the Snipe, and in May 1959 the trolleybus terminus was moved back to the gates of Ryecroft Hall, offices of Audenshaw Urban District Council, in Manchester Road. A siding was installed to allow through buses to overtake 215 and 218x short workings. On 11 June 1966, Ashton 86, working through on the 218, passes Manchester 1342 taking standing time on the 215.
Peter Thompson

From 26th November 1959, trolleybuses used the new Stalybridge bus station. Ashton 77, two Manchester BUTs and plenty of passengers, on a miserably wet day in March 1963. The bus station was flanked by some fine examples of three-storey 'piece-work' weaver's cottages.
Ted Jones

Haughton Green, until this time a quiet backwater, was chosen for one of the city's large new overspill housing estates. There would be several thousand new homes and most of the new residents would require transport to the city. Services would need to be extended and modified as the estate developed. The 217 trolleybus to Ashton would hardly serve and it was quickly agreed to replace it with motor buses. The remaining 27 of the 1100 batch were due for replacement and it would be reasonable to offset these against the 213 and 217 conversions. Interestingly, new motor buses to replace the trolleybuses were never specially ordered and were simply included as part of the normal programme of fleet replacement.

This showed that the trolleybuses were finished, for they could very easily have provided the city service — the wiring from Haughton Green to the city existed and only a short extension in Haughton Green was necessary.

The 213 service was converted on 1st June 1959, the last trolleybus running on Sunday 31st May. Before that there was a unique occasion when an Ashton BUT trolleybus was hired by enthusiasts and toured the Miller Street section and other parts of the Manchester system. The replacement motor bus service followed the same route apart from the Withy Grove diversion, its service number (123) being a neat remix of its trolleybus number.

The Haughton Green service lasted about a year longer, the gap largely caused by delays in deliveries of new buses. Ashton's new Leyland PD2s having arrived, the last 217 ran on 3rd July 1960, 1359 working the final journey. Buses took over next day, the service renumbered 127 in similar manner to the 213.

The passing of the 217 probably caused more regret than any other conversion save the last one, for the route had a distinctive atmosphere. Quiet and in parts semi rural, the road to Haughton Green literally ended in the village. It prompted one to imagine that, if it could have had feelings, the trolleybus standing quietly in the lay-by near the church welcomed the peace and quiet before its next day's work, heavily loaded and jostling with cars, vans, lorries and other buses in the city centre.

In May 1959, 1329 on Upper Lloyd Street going to Greenheys. Trimbel Brothers' fish, poultry and greengrocery shop is offering fresh chickens, cod and plaice at 2 shillings (10p) a pound; salmon, then a more expensive fish, was 5 shillings (25p), apples and Jersey new potatoes were one shilling (5p). It seems cheap but when converted to 2007 money values the true cost is about the same.
Peter Caunt

A new 'overspill' housing estate brought the end of the 217 and of Haughton Green as a quiet backwater. Ashton's Bond-rebodied Sunbeam 63 approaching Haughton Green terminus on one of the last journeys in July 1960.
OTA/ Chris Bennett/ Martin Jenkins

Ashton's four-wheel Streamliners were withdrawn over a six-year period. 54 was one of the last, by which time some rebuilding work had been done on the side windows and a new front grille fitted, although there was still no service number indicator. Portland Street, 29th April 1959 with 1162.
J. S. Cockshott Archive

Manchester Corporation Transport Department.

GREENHEYS AND CORPORATION STREET - Service No. 213.

On Monday, 1st June 1959, this service will be converted from trolleybus to motorbus operation and will be renumbered No 123.

The route will be as at present to Swan Street via Shudehill, Withy Grove to and along Corporation Street returning via Miller Street and as at present.

A fifteen minute service, with the present starting and finishing times, will be operated, with augmentation to the present frequency during peak periods.

Sunday Service every twenty minutes.

A handbill will be available giving service times.

A. F. NEAL, General Manager.

The Moston services converted, all but 27 of the prewar fleet were sold for scrap. Aluminium and Allied Products Ltd was the rather grand title of one of the scrap dealers that bought the first to go. At its Globe Lane, Dukinfield, yard in 1956 are 1077, which had not run since 1951, and two others.
Peter Caunt

Inflation — Fares 1939-1966

The fares in the tables are in "old", pre-decimalisation pence and shillings:- 12 old pence (12d) = one shilling (1/-) = 5 new pence (5p). Inflation was rife in the 1960s and it is interesting to compare the fares with those of 2007, for the 219 service was still operating in 2007, the fare from Piccadilly to Guide Bridge on Stagecoach's service being £2.00. In real money values (what £1 would buy), 1/- in 1939 was the equivalent of about £2.00 in 2007.

This picture of Stagecoach 19076, an Alexander Dennis Enviro400, taken on 14th March 2007, has some nice touches of nostalgia. In the background the old Corporation Transport headquarters at 55 Piccadilly still stands, long since converted to an hotel; the bus is passing the former 219 trolleybus terminus in Portland Street and is operating from Hyde Road Garage.
Mike Shaw

1939 Picadilly–Guide Bridge 3½d

```
Guide Bridge
  1d   Lumb Lane
  1d   1d   Fairfield Office or Audenshaw Road
  1½d  1d   1d   Fairfield Road or Gransmoor Road
  2d   1½d  1d   1d   Wellington Street (Higher Openshaw)
  2d   1½d  1½d  1d   1d   Grey Mare Lane
  2½d  2d   2d   1½d  1d   1d   Viaduct Street
  3d   2½d  2½d  2d   1½d  1d   1d   Mayfield Station
  3½d  3d   3d   2½d  2d   1½d  1d   1d   Piccadilly
```

1948 Picadilly–Guide Bridge 5d

SERVICE No. 29.—PICCADILLY and ASHTON via GUIDE BRIDGE.

Piccadilly
1½d	Mayfield Station
1½d	1½d	Chancery Lane or Viaduct Street
2d	1½d	1½d	Gresham Street
2½d	2d	1½d	1½d	Clayton Lane
3d	2½d	2d	1½d	1½d	Wellington Street
3d	3d	2½d	2d	1½d	1½d	Lees Street or Fairfield Road
	3d	3d	2½d	2d	1½d	1½d	Fairfield Office
		3d	3d	2½d	2d	1½d	1½d	Audenshaw Road (Manchester Road)
4d			3d	3d	2½d	2d	1½d	1½d	Lumb Lane
5d	4d	4d	4d	3d	3d	2½d	2d	1½d	1½d	Guide Bridge
6d	5d	5d	5d	4d	4d	3½d	3d	2½d	2d	1d	Trafalgar Square
6d	5d	5d	5d	4d	4d	3½d	3d	2½d	2½d	1d	1d	Chester Square
6½d	5½d	5½d	5½d	4½d	4½d	4d	3½d	3d	3d	1½d	1d	1d	Cavendish Street
6½d	5½d	5½d	5½d	4½d	4½d	4d	3½d	3d	3d	1½d	1½d	1d	1d	Ashton (Market Place)

Minimum fare from Piccadilly during evening and Saturday noon rush hours.................4d.

SUPPLEMENTARY FARE :
Workmen's Return Fare (before 8.0 a.m.)
Ashton and Guide Bridge........................2d

Supplementary Children's ½d. Half-fare :
Coronation Square and Fairfield Office.

Manchester Corporation Regulations for children's fares apply between Piccadilly and Guide Bridge.

1958 Picadilly–Guide Bridge 6d

SERVICE No. 219.—PICCADILLY and ASHTON (via Guide Bridge)

Stage Nos.

01	Piccadilly (Portland Street)									
02	2d	Mayfield Station								
03	2d	2d	Chancellor Lane or Viaduct Street							
04	3d	2d	2d	Gresham Street						
05	4d	3d	2d	2d	Clayton Lane					
06	4d	4d	3d	2d	2d	Beulah Street				
07	5d	4d	4d	3d	2d	2d	Louisa Street or Fairfield Road			
08	5d	5d	4d	4d	3d	2d	2d	Fairfield Office		
09	6d	5d	5d	4d	4d	3d	2d	2d	Audenshaw Road (Manchester Road)	
10	6d	6d	5d	5d	4d	4d	3d	2d	2d	Lumb Lane
11	6d	6d	6d	5d	5d	4d	4d	3d	2d	2d	Guide Bridge
12	7½d	7½d	7½d	6½d	6½d	5½d	5½d	4½d	3d	3d	2d	Trafalgar Square
13	8d	8d	8d	7d	7d	6d	6d	5d	4d	3½d	2d	2d	Chester Square
14	8½d	8½d	8½d	7½d	7½d	6½d	6½d	5½d	4d	3½d	2½d	2d	2d	Cavendish Street
15	8½d	8½d	8½d	7½d	7½d	6½d	6½d	5½d	4d	3½d	2½d	2½d	2d	2d	Ashton (Market Place)

M.C.T.D. Early Morning Fares available between Piccadilly and Guide Bridge.

Early Morning Single Fare
(before 8 a.m.)
Ashton and Guide Bridge 2d

On Journeys to Ashton only.

Minimum Fare of 5d until arrival at Mayfield Station between 4-30 and 6-20 p.m. Monday to Friday, and 12 noon and 1-0 p.m. on Saturday.

Manchester Corporation Regulations apply between Piccadilly and Guide Bridge.
Ashton Corporation Regulations apply between Guide Bridge and Ashton.

1966 Picadilly–Guide Bridge 1/-

SERVICE No. 219.—PICCADILLY and ASHTON (via Guide Bridge)

Stage Nos.

01	Piccadilly (Portland Street) (01)									
02	3	Mayfield Station (02)								
03	4	3	Chancellor Lane (03)							
04	6	4	3	Gresham Street (04)						
05	6	6	4	3	Clayton Lane (05)					
06	9	6	6	4	3	Beulah Street (06)				
07	9	9	6	6	4	3	Louisa Street or Fairfield Road (07)			
08	9	9	9	6	6	4	3	Fairfield Office (08)		
09	9	9	9	9	6	6	4	3	Audenshaw Road (Manchester Road) (09)	
10	1/-	9	9	9	9	6	6	4	3	Lumb Lane (10)
11	1/-	1/-	9	9	9	9	6	6	4	3	Guide Bridge (11)
12	1/-	1/-	1/-	9	9	9	9	6	6	4	3	Trafalgar Square (12)
13	1/-	1/-	1/-	9	9	9	9	7	6	6	3	3	Chester Square (13)
14	1/-	1/-	1/-	1/-	1/-	9	9	9	8	6	4	3	3	Globe Hotel, Cavendish Street (14)
15	1/2	1/-	1/-	1/-	1/-	9	9	9	8	7	4	4	3	3	Ashton (Bus Station) (15)

Manchester Corporation Regulations apply between Piccadilly and Guide Bridge.
Ashton Corporation Regulations apply between Guide Bridge and Ashton.

Cheap Travel Tickets available between Piccadilly and Guide Bridge

Aytoun Street at 23.04hrs on 10th October 1964; 1345 works the final trolleybus journey on the 219, a short to Guide Bridge. There was no public announcement of the changeover.
Peter Thompson

The next service to go was the 210 — the 213 and 217 report had mentioned that it might be necessary to consider its future, again due to the changing pattern of housing. A large 'overspill' estate was being built at Hattersley, on the Glossop road between Hyde and Mottram, which Manchester and SHMD intended to serve jointly. This plan was disrupted by the North Western Road Car Company's claiming a share of the traffic. The result was an argument outside the scope of this book but one that made the introduction of services as urgent as did the growing number of completed new homes.

This caused problems for Ashton. It had raised the question of the future of the trolleybuses in 1953, stating that it would keep them for at least ten years. In September of 1958, however, it had asked Manchester for a date for conversion because if there was no prospect of early replacement, it would have to consider the purchase of second-hand vehicles, possibly from Brighton. Manchester remained unsympathetic. Although conversion was far off, Ashton did not buy any second-hand vehicles, making do with its eight new BUTs and the four wartime Sunbeams that had been fitted with new bodies in 1954/55 and 1958.

In 1961, the ten years were nearly up and Ashton wanted decisions. In July it asked Manchester for an early start upon the conversion of its services. A start was to be made on a new by-pass road involving a large roundabout at Chester Square and the expense of new overhead with possibly only a short life was of great concern. At the time Manchester's Transport and City Surveyor's Departments (the latter responsible for the city's roads) were indeed discussing the end of the trolleybus system but their priorities lay elsewhere. Ashton was told that there was little prospect of an early conversion of its services. An unhappy Ashton continued to urge, raising concerns in October about the restrictions of the trolleybus system on the new town centre and bus station developments. It did not want to divert the trolleybuses into the new bus station because of the costs but, as it stood, the overhead was in the way.

As a result in November 1961 the Department produced a by now familiar report. One hundred and two vehicles were required for service (210 — 28, 215 — 21, 216 -19, 218 — 15, 219 -19). By 1st April 1962 the loan debt on the 1200- and 1240-series would be cleared. They had been overhauled in 1955 and 1956 and were due for a costly second overhaul; the overhead would require heavy expenditure and the loan taken out on the BUT vehicles would be repaid in 1967. If final conversion was planned for 1967 the 1200- and 1240-

series could be withdrawn in 1963, the BUTs would receive a minimal overhaul and overhead expenditure could be reduced to 'care and maintenance'. Pressure from the joint operators (coyly, no names were mentioned) could bring the date earlier. This was approved by the City Council on 6th December and Ashton and SHMD were informed.

Immediately, plans were made to convert the 210 early in 1963. Ashton Corporation's reaction to this news was one of extreme displeasure. The two operators met to argue the matter in February. Ashton wanted early abandonment of its services instead of or as well as the Gee Cross service but delivery times for new buses were lengthy and Manchester's priority was to serve Hattersley and curb North Western's ambitions. All Ashton achieved was a small concession that the conversion of the 219 would be accelerated so that the layout at Chester Square could be simpler.

The 210 was progressively changed to motor buses. Peak hour duties first, then after 19th January 1963 alternate service journeys were operated by motor buses, their short workings to Hyde using the new bus station instead of running on to Smithy Lane. On the same weekend the Saturday afternoon trolleybus operation of the service to Denton ceased — it had been the province of six-wheelers 1240-1255. The last trolleybus journeys were on the evening of 28th April 1963, 1331 operating the last full trip to Gee Cross followed by 1308 on the final journey inwards from Smithy Lane to Hyde Road garage.

The remaining 1200s and 1240s were kept in service to cover for the overhaul programme on the BUTs and were withdrawn as the latter emerged from the

---

The 210 service was always first choice for the postwar Crossleys and few BUTs operated on it, mainly towards the end. In February 1963, 1310 passes Debdale Park; in the background is Gorton Bridge which carries the road over the abandoned Stockport Branch of the Ashton Canal.
Peter Thompson

Gee Cross on 24th March 1963 when the 210 was part motor bus and part trolleybus operated. Ten-year-old Northern Counties-bodied Leyland PD2 3310 had been transferred from Parrs Wood garage to Hyde Road for the work. The last 210 trolleybus ran at the end of April.
Peter Thompson

Construction of Mancunian Way caused the removal of the overhead wiring in Downing Street, trolleybuses then having to use Great Ancoats Street to take up service. The Ardwick Green power feeder was scheduled to be disconnected from 24th May 1965 but the work seems to have been delayed. Five days later the work had been done but by some mishap in communication 1329 and 1328 starting a mid-day duty, took the Ardwick Green route, ran onto the disconnected section and became stranded. They were towed into the city by the Department's Ford Thames Trader, A74.
Peter Thompson

Car Works' paint shop, the last in October 1963. SHMD's remaining mile or so of overhead in Stalybridge was taken over for maintenance by Ashton.

On Saturday 10th October 1964 with no notice to the general public, trolleybus operation of the 219 ceased, motor buses taking over the following day. As with the 210 the service number was not changed. The last full journey by Ashton was worked by BUT 88 and Manchester's last full journey by 1304. The final journey on the route was by 1345 on the 23.30 journey from Guide Bridge to Hyde Road garage. Ashton quickly removed the overhead from Chester Square to Guide Bridge. The Chester Square roadworks had already commenced with bizarre arrangements for the 216 and 218 trolleybuses to run through the middle of the contractor's site, thereby avoiding altering the overhead until the new road was completed.

Conversion of the 215 and 216 began on 19th July 1964 when the all-night trolleybuses on 215x were replaced by buses. Also during this month trolleybuses ceased to work on Sundays on the 218 and 219, motor buses taking their place,

allowing maintenance rosters to be simplified. There was one small piece of new wiring — construction of Mancunian Way involved a new roundabout at Fairfield Street; the inward track for the 212, 218 and 219 was altered to go around this from 27th July, the outward track being changed on 18th October ready for operation the next day, by which time the 219 had ceased.

Some of the BUTs were now surplus but only two (1317, 1344) were withdrawn, in July. Before that 1346 had been scrapped after hitting a traction pole in North Road late in 1961, its driver trying to avoid a swerving car. 1360 had been withdrawn in April 1964 after being run into by no less an historic vehicle than SHMD's unique Atkinson double-decker, number 70.

In December 1964 22 BUTs were withdrawn; most were towed to Birchfields Road garage for undercover storage. There was some thought of their possible sale elsewhere but no interest emerged and they were used as a source of spares — their seats were removed and fitted to Daimlers 4480-4489 and Leyland Atlanteans 3621-3630, replacing their original lightweight

but uncomfortable low-backed seats.

Construction of the junction of Mancunian Way and Downing Street caused removal of the link for garage journeys from Piccadilly via Downing Street, Ardwick Green and Hyde Road during the week of 24th May 1965. In Ashton the roundabout at Chester Square was completed, Ashton installed new overhead and it opened on 12th April 1965.

Manchester's General Manager, Albert Neal, retired in March 1965; his successor, Ralph Bennett, inherited the dying trolleybus system. In May 1966, as a result of the shorter working week for crews, Manchester stopped working trolleybuses on the 218. Manchester's only operations were then the basic weekday Ashton New Road 215 and 216 plus a few weekend turns. Ashton continued to work its duties on the Ashton Old Road 218 with trolleybuses. Everything else was diesel. In October one of the Guy tower wagons was sold to Blackpool Corporation.

On 13th July 1966, with delivery of sufficient new buses in prospect, Ralph Bennett proposed that the final

In December 1964, 22 of the BUTs were withdrawn and most were towed to undercover storage in Birchfields Road garage. It was hoped that one of the few remaining trolleybus operators might show some interest in buying them but there was none. 1361, 1347, 1340 and 1338.
John Dugdale via Keith Walker

The Ashton by-pass involved a new roundabout at Chester Square, its construction causing traffic diversions though side streets. It was impractical to put up temporary wiring with the bizarre result that, until the new junction was opened on 12th April 1965, the trolleybuses continued to use their existing route right through the middle of the road works, negotiating excavators, dumpers, oil drums and sundry piles of rubble. 1332 on 9th April 1965.
Peter Thompson

abandonment be at the end of December — a date quickly approved by all concerned. On 27th August, Saturday working by trolleybuses ceased; an exception was an enthusiasts' tour on Saturday 3rd September using 1325. In November the wires in Newton Street (from Hilton Street), London Road to Fairfield Street, the Portland Street sidings, the Aytoun Street siding and loops at Fairfield Road and The Trough were

removed. It was announced that the final day of operation would be Friday, 30th December 1966.

Trolleybuses remained a sensitive issue in the city and there would be no formal civic ceremonies. Ashton's last vehicle would be decorated with posters and Manchester would produce an illustrated full colour window poster for display in the buses. On the day after closure, Manchester would leave power on and provide support staff

On 27th December 1966, Ashton 87, already decorated for its final trip on the 30th, was hired for an enthusiasts' tour. Photographed in Ashton garage forecourt, the tour was solely on Ashton's wires.
Don Jones

for two preserved trolleybuses to run enthusiasts' tours over its part of the system.

With its vehicle pictures, Manchester's window poster would have been rather fine and without doubt a collector's item. Sadly, a strike at the printers prevented its being produced, with the unhappy result that the only intimation that the trolleybuses were to finish was a printed notice in, of all things, Mayne's buses. The reason for this apparently strange occurrence was that Mayne's service to Kershaw Lane was to be absorbed into Manchester's new limited stop bus service 214 (Stevenson Square — Ashton New Road — Audenshaw) with Mayne then operating all the journeys on service 46 (Stevenson Square — Droylsden), which was to be renumbered 213.

The last day started with drizzling rain, the sides of the buses becoming covered with spray and road dirt. Although the roads were still damp, the evening turned fine encouraging a fair number of people to have a final trolleybus ride. Ashton's last vehicles were 83, which had been in service all day, followed by specially decorated 87, on the 22.27hrs 218 from Piccadilly to Stalybridge returning to Ashton Market and Mossley Road garage. Both carried a full load, including Ashton's Chairman and General Manager on 87; Manchester officials and staff remained anonymous.

The timetabled late journeys on Ashton Old Road were all scheduled to be worked by Manchester motorbuses. To everyone's surprise and with a nice sense of occasion, Hyde Road garage turned out a nicely-cleaned 1302 to work the 22.52 218x to Ryecroft Hall, returning at 23.20 thence to Hyde Road garage. Thus the oldest trolleybus bus in the fleet became the last public trolleybus along the Old Road.

On Ashton New Road, the final departure was the 23.00hrs 215 from Stevenson Square to Ryecroft Hall and back thence to Hyde Road garage. Anticipating a crowd, Manchester provided a duplicate — 1321 which ran in front of 1354. Filled to capacity the two trolleybuses ran to Audenshaw and back to Hyde Road garage. Drivers of other buses, Mayne's included, flashed a salute on their headlamps as they passed. When 1354 turned into the Bennett Street entrance to Hyde Road garage and works at 23.50hrs on 30th December 1966, public operation of trolleybuses in Manchester came to an end.

On the following day, the Department kindly allowed the former Manchester 1344 and Rotherham 44, both preserved and in sparkling condition, to operate enthusiasts' tours over Manchester's wires. When the preserved 1344 entered Hyde Road at 20.00hrs on New Year's Eve 1966, the power was turned off. Fifteen new Daimler Fleetlines, 4746-4760, entered service at Hyde Road on 1st January and all that remained was to sell the withdrawn trolleybuses for scrap and take down the overhead wiring The wires at Hyde Road garage were taken down by the Department's staff and the rest by contractors Thos. W. Ward & Co Ltd of Sheffield. The remaining tower wagons were sold, the 1947 Thornycroft into preservation, the Guy joining its sister vehicle with Blackpool Corporation.

Not so in Stalybridge, where there was an argument which somehow typified the story of the Manchester trolleybus network. The long drawn out dispute was whether Ashton or SHMD was responsible for removing the overhead in Stalybridge, which SHMD owned but which had passed to Ashton for maintenance purposes in 1963. The argument dragged on for well over a year and the wiring was still in place in March 1968. The dispute was then resolved by royal intervention — an impending visit to Stalybridge by Her Majesty the Queen causing swift action.

Right: The final public trolleybus on Ashton Old Road was the 22.52hrs 218x Portland Street to Audenshaw. The turn would normally have been worked by a motor bus but, to mark the last public journey along Ashton Old Road, Hyde Road turned out the oldest trolleybus, 1302 which is entering Hyde Road garage at 23.42hrs.
Peter Thompson

Below: The final public journey was on Ashton New Road and was the 23.00hrs 215 from Stevenson Square to Audenshaw and back to Hyde Road garage, worked by 1354 duplicated in front by 1321. 1354 is in Stevenson Square about to pull onto the stand for the final departure.
Peter Thompson

Arrivals at Hyde Road

Time	Bus	Service
23.04	1357	216x
23.42	1302	218x
23.43	1321, 1336	215
23.50	1354	215

The final public journeys, Friday December 30th

Service	Timetabled at	from	to	bus	comment
216	21.36	Stevenson Square	Stalybridge	1354	last 216 to Stalybridge
216x	22.06	Stevenson Square	Ashton	1357	last 216 to Ashton
216	22.20	Stalybridge	Stevenson Square	1354	last full journey on 216
218	22.27	Piccadilly	Stalybridge	83, 87	last Ashton trolleybus, 83 in front of 87
216x	22.40	Ashton	Hyde Road garage	1357	last 216
218x	22.52	Piccadilly	Audenshaw	1302	MCT specially operate 1302, last public trolleybus on Ashton Old Road
215	22.56	Stevenson Square	Audenshaw	1336	
215	23.00	Stevenson Square	Audenshaw	1321, 1354	final outward journey, 1321 ahead of 1354
218	23.07	Stalybridge	Ashton garage	83, 87	final Ashton Corporation journey, 83 ahead of 87
218x	23.20	Audenshaw	Hyde Road garage	1302	final public journey on Ashton Old Road
216	23.23	Audenshaw	Hyde Road garage	1336	
215	23.28	Audenshaw	Hyde Road garage	1321, 1354	final public journey on the system, Ashton New Road, 1321 ahead of 1354

Above: 15th May 1959 was a bright sunny day when John Kaye took this splendid picture of Crossleys 1167 and 1169 at Portland Street terminus, about to be overtaken by Stockport Leyland PD2 277. Both trolleybuses look smart and 1169 would run for a further 10 months but 1167 would be withdrawn at the end of May.
John Kaye

Below: Equally smart-looking 1166 leaving Beck Street at the Fairfield Road turn-back on a rush-hour inwards short working to the Fire Station, London Road in 1959. It was the final Streamliner trolleybus to be withdrawn, in September 1960.
OTA/Chris Bennett

Crossley 1155 on the 213 and Leyland 1100 on the 215x pass the Daily Express Building in Great Ancoats Street. Completed in 1939, the glass-fronted building was one of the sights of Manchester and as good an example of the 'Modern' architectural movement as one could find. The printing presses in the triple-height press hall were an impressive sight from the street, particularly at night when at work and brightly illuminated.
Photobus — Jim Copland

On a warm summer Sunday afternoon in the late 1950s, Crossley 'Empire' 1216 waits at the 210 terminus in George Street. Behind the bus, a vendor sells ice cream from a hand-pushed cart. Barratt's shoe shop and Littlewoods store 'for value' are in the background.
Don Jones

Outbound on the 210 on Hyde Road, near Belle Vue, 1200 is followed by Salford Daimler 439 on the cross-city 77 service. The large windscreens were a feature of the 1200-series but became draughty and prone to leaks and the nearside unit was replaced by fixed glazing on overhaul. February 1962. *John Ryan*

A well-known face. 1242 at Thornley Park turn-back at Easter 1962, on an enthusiasts' tour organised by Cliff Taylor, who is walking round the corner of the bus. A diligent and thorough tramway researcher and historian, and co-author of the 1967 book, Cliff lived to see the realisation of his chief ambition, the preserved tramway in Heaton Park.
Photobus — Arnold Richardson

At Crown Point, Denton, the 217 service crossed the route of the 210. Crossley 1211 draws up to a typical MCT concrete-framed shelter at the stop in Stockport Road. Alongside is overhead feeder box 71, the trunking for the power cables running up the adjacent pole.
OTA/Chris Bennett

Early in 1963, three 1200-series are on
Market Street near Lumn Road, Hyde,
bound for Piccadilly. The front vehicle is
1204, the centre vehicle is unidentified
but the third is 1203, recognisable by
being the only 1200-series vehicle to be
repainted in the so-called 'all-red' livery;
a job done somewhat unexpectedly in
1961 after accident damage.
*B. Goodfellow via Howard Piltz
collection*

Blue sky and the houses on Joel Lane,
going up to Werneth Low, form the
backdrop for this east-facing long shot
of Gee Cross terminus in 1962. The
trolleybuses are 1229 and 1204.
OTA/Chris Bennett

In December 1962, 1216 stands at the
Gee Cross terminus which was
somewhat curiously situated on the
apex of the junction of Dowson Road
and Stockport Road.
Photobus — Arnold Richardson

Above: With its white lining out, Ashton's red, white and blue livery looked particularly smart when new. Crossley 'Empire' 80 in Old Square, Ashton.
Photobus — Jim Copland

Below: Ashton's colourful livery could become dull when weathered and in this case is not enhanced by Crossley 'Empire'

78's black side advertisement panel. The contract for the painted-on advertisement had expired and the space was painted black until the new advertising contract was agreed. Advertisements were a source of useful income at a time when passenger numbers were falling but there was no question of displaying one which was not being paid for.
Don Jones

In 1954 Ashton appointed a new general manager, Terence O'Donnell, previously general manager at Yorkshire company operator Mexborough and Swinton, part of the large BET group. Managerial moves between companies and municipalities were very unusual but in this case there was good reason as Mexborough and Swinton had operated trolleybuses. He introduced a bright new peacock blue and cream livery. Crossley 77 turning into Aytoun Street on 16th April 1959.
John Kaye

Tickets

Both operators used similar ticketing systems which were of the same type as the motor buses. The first were Bell Punch — a different colour for each fare, carried in a rack by the guard who punched a hole to show the stage. In 1939 a 1d ride (one halfpenny for children) would take you from Denton to Haughton Green, it was 3d to the Gardener's Arms and 3½d would buy a ride from Piccadilly to Guide Bridge. In 1948 the lowest adult fare was 1½d, a trip to the Gardener's Arms from town cost 4d and Guide Bridge was 5d (12d (old pence) = 1 shilling = 5p).

In 1950 the 'Ultimate' machine was introduced at Rochdale Road and Hyde Road, Ashton following suit in the same year. This machine, also made by the Bell Punch Company, issued smaller square tickets. It held either five or six types of tickets, the machines being known as the five-barrel or six-barrel model; multiple tickets were issued for higher fares. The lowest adult fare was 2d, Denton to Haughton Green was 3d; Piccadilly to Guide Bridge was 6d (2 x 3d tickets) as was a trip from Piccadilly to Denton on the 210.

Many of Ashton Corporation Passenger Transport's Bell Punch and Ultimate tickets were supplied by the well-known Ashton firm of Alfred Williamson & Son Ltd, which had a substantial business supplying tickets to railway, bus and tram operators across the United Kingdom and beyond, although it received very little business from Manchester.

In 1963 Manchester began to change over to the 'Setright' machine which issued oblong white tickets, printed in the machine. This 1965 one shilling ticket would buy a ride from Piccadilly to Guide Bridge.
Michael Eyre

Body maker Burlingham took only black and white pictures of the 1300-series but this picture of preserved 1344 in Hyde Road garage on 30th December 1966, newly restored and repainted for its tour on the day after the trolleybus system closed for public operation, shows what they looked like when new. It is now in the care of the East Anglia Transport Museum at Carlton Colville.
Howard Piltz

The new BUTs looked smart with black mudguards, brown edging and cream round the upper-deck windows. Six-months-old 1357 with prewar Manchester and Ashton streamliner Crossleys at the 'old' Portland Street terminus in late summer 1956.
Don Jones

1326 on the 210 alongside Ashton 81 on the 218 at the "new" terminus in Portland Street. At the Queens Hotel, a van is delivering 'G-Plan' furniture, a design icon of the 1960s. During the 1950s, the poles supporting the overhead in the city centre were painted grey instead of the usual green. *OTA/Chris Bennett*

There was a problem with the paint that Burlingham used on some of the BUTs and a few had to be repainted after only two years. It is evident on the cream band above the windscreen on this shot of 1332 at Crown Point, Denton, bound for Haughton Green. *OTA/Chris Bennett*

Overhaul of some of the 1300-series was delayed whilst the future of the trolleybus system was decided and those so affected began to look somewhat run-down, as here on 1341 at the junction of Old Street and Crickets Lane, Ashton, early in 1963. 1341 was soon smart once more, being spray-painted 'all-red' in May. *John Ryan*

Spray painting was economical but paint masking techniques meant that 'everything not glass' got sprayed red; the only relief was the single cream band. In this early rush-hour picture of Stevenson Square on a rainy day in 1965, Leyland PD2 3435 leaves on the 2x for the Boat and Horses on the Chadderton boundary; BUT 1342 is going only as far as Edge Lane and the queue, headed by the man reading the *Manchester Evening News*, is waiting for the Stalybridge-bound 216 behind. Louis Gross's *'clothing for all the family, direct to the public at warehouse prices'* shop was a feature of the square.
OTA/Reg Wilson

The line of Morris Commercial Royal Mail vans is outside what was then the city's main sorting office in Newton Street. Fully laden and with standing passengers, 1304 is turning into Hilton Street and Stevenson Square; one passenger is about to jump off the platform to save having to walk back from the square. The sides of the bus are covered in grime from the day's work on damp winter roads.
Howard Piltz

Also dirty from wet roads, 1308 turns from Oldham Street into Great Ancoats Street at New Cross, outbound on a 215 to Audenshaw. An Austin Mini, an Austin Farina-style A60 and a Warburton's bread van wait at the lights. In the background is the CIS skyscraper, built on the site of the terminus of the former 213 trolleybus service.
Howard Piltz

The 'all-red' livery was applied by spraying
hot paint in a closed booth. The process
saved time and money, and with falling
passenger numbers such cost savings were
essential. The Department tried various
types of paint but all dulled quickly. Newly
repainted in mid-1963, 1361 and 1308 in
Portland Street still have a gloss about
them.
Tony Belton

Manchester's last new
trolleybus towards the
end of its life: 1362
outbound on Ashton
New Road in 1966. In the
background are two
long-since-nationalised
former enterprises of the
City of Manchester: the
chimneys and cooling
towers of Stuart Street
Power Station and the
gas holders of Bradford
Road Gas Works.
Howard Piltz

Even though a co-ordination agreement
was reached in 1957, Mayne's buses
continued to be very different from
those of the Corporation. In this 1966
picture, Mayne's new 30-foot long East
Lancashire-bodied AEC Regent, CXJ
522C, in-bound on the 46 from
Greenside Lane to the city, is coming
out of Manor Road, passing the
Department's mock half-timbered Edge
Lane traffic and parcels office. The
lights are green for the trolleybus but
Mayne had much local support and
some passengers will allow BUT 1330 to
pass and wait for 'the Mayne's'.
Howard Piltz

In 1957 Ashton bought new Roe-bodies for 1944 Sunbeams 61 and 62; traction batteries and low voltage lighting were also fitted. They re-entered service in January 1958 but although they had had this costly rebuild and had years of life left, they were taken out of service at the end of 1965. There was no second-hand interest and they went for scrap.
Photobus — Arnold Richardson

Somewhat unexpectedly, Ashton 80 became the longest lasting of the postwar Crossley trolleybuses. Manchester and Ashton withdrew their final ones in 1963 but Ashton then needed an extra vehicle to work off an imbalance of mileage between the two operators and 80 was returned to service, running until the end of October 1964. This picture was taken in August. The bus passed into preservation and is now in the Greater Manchester Museum of Transport.
Howard Piltz

Platforms 13/14 at Piccadilly (formerly London Road) station were first famous as the terminus of the Manchester South Junction and Altrincham electric trains. Latterly they have become the 'through' platform by which trains from the south reach the routes to the north of the city and vice versa. In this picture, taken from the junction of London Road and Fairfield Street in 1965, Ashton 84 is inbound on the 218 and Manchester Leyland PD2 3367 outbound on the 219, converted the previous October. The brick wall on the left has some contemporary political graffiti.
Howard Piltz

There was a convenient exit from
Platforms 13/14 via a set of steps to
Fairfield Street and the bus stop. 1328
on the 218 picks up passengers in
mid-1965.
OTA/M. Taylor

At Pin Mill Brow, Ardwick, the wiring for
the 213 service crossed Ashton Old Road,
remaining in place for trolleybuses
working to and from Hyde Road garage
after the 213 ended. 1334 has finished its
turn on the 215 and is going back to
garage. Swerling's Chemist and Optician is
a splendid example of the now-vanished
small shop. Signs of this are already there
— Wilson Brothers' paint and wallpaper
shop has closed.
OTA/Reg Wilson

On Ashton Old Road just beyond Pin
Mill Brow, Ashton BUT 89 on the 219
pulls away from the stop; the passenger
is waiting for either a 21 motor bus to
Dukinfield or 218 trolleybus.
OTA/Reg Wilson

Above: When the terminus was moved from the Snipe to Ryecroft Hall, the destination blinds were altered simply to read 'Audenshaw', although some timetables still referred to the Snipe. 1324 is at the siding wiring at an island on the gyratory system. Located 50 or so yards before the terminus itself, this allowed trolleybuses on 215 or 218x to pass each other should they arrive in the wrong sequence for departure. There was a further siding at Ryecroft Hall which allowed through 216s and 218s to pass buses standing at the terminus.
OTA/Reg Wilson

Left: It is one of the last times that the guard will pull the rope handle to switch a trolleybus into Ryecroft Hall siding, for this is the afternoon of the final day of operation, 1301 is in obviously run-down condition and dirty with grime from earlier rain. The 'go by bus' posters are a strange juxtaposition with the lower advert for Volkswagen agent William Arnold Ltd, Based in Upper Brook Street, Arnold's was a long-established firm which, in the late 1920s and early 1930s, was well known for building high-quality car bodies on Rolls Royce, Bentley, Daimler and Crossley chassis. In 1930 it built a few bus bodies including six double-deckers for Manchester but found motor car work more profitable.
OTA/Reg Wilson

Above right: Trolleybuses to Stalybridge stopped alongside Ashton's Market Hall. Smartly painted Ashton 83 leaves on the 218 in 1963. Behind it, food for the sweet-toothed is being delivered from the van of C. Kunzle Ltd, Birmingham, makers of fine cakes.
Tony Belton

Right: Carrying a good load of passengers on a wet summer's day in 1966, 1308 turns from Bow Street into Market Street, Ashton. The guard, wearing his summer dust jacket, stands on the platform's edge to stare at the photographer.
OTA/Chris Bennett

At dusk on a winter afternoon in December 1965, Ashton 89 has its interior lights on at Stamford Square as it passes Beaufort Road en route to Stalybridge.
OTA/Reg Wilson

Bound for Stevenson Square, 1323 has just passed the county boundary sign at Stamford Park and stopped at the large Victorian cast iron-framed shelter, erected in tramway days. The paintwork of the overhead poles changes from SHMD grey to Ashton's green and the poles have two white bands, indicating the section break in the overhead wiring. The bus carries an advert for C&A, the large fashion store in Manchester's Oldham Street, just down the street from Stevenson Square. Summer 1964.
Tony Belton

An impatiently-driven Land Rover squeezes between SHMD's Leyland PD2 fleet number 1 (101 UTU) bound for Manchester on limited stop service 6 from Glossop and 1356 coming down Rassbottom Street towards Stalybridge, its driver having already changed the destination ready for the inward journey.
Tony Belton

Above: Hyde Road crews' blind settings were not at their best when Tony Belton took this and the previous picture in 1964. Newly-repainted 1320 is about to pass under the railway at Stalybridge station; it is working the 216 but the crew has left the service number set to 215. On the other side of the road is a poster hanger with handcart, ladders and paste pots.
Tony Belton

Below: Some of the arches of the railway viaduct along Waterloo Road were the base of long-established Kitson's Coaches. Its June 1963 spray paint still shiny, 1320 passes Leyland Royal Tiger ODH 721 in the red livery of Kitson's subsidiary Gee Cross Coaches. Like 1320, the coach has a Burlingham body: the firm's 'Seagull' design was one of the most stylish coaches of the 1950s.
Tony Belton

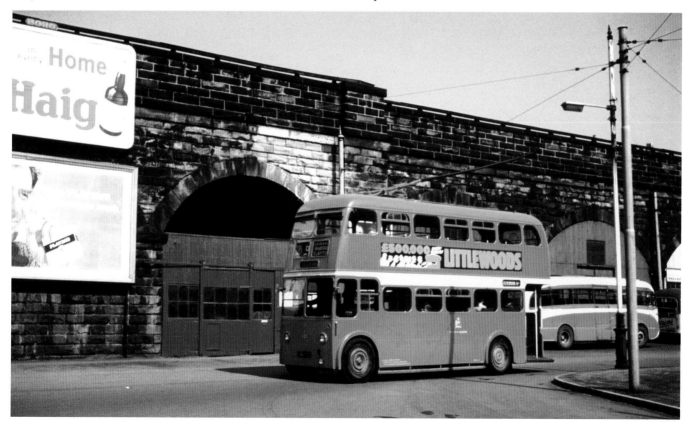

Five buses but no passengers. Manchester and Ashton trolleybuses and SHMD Daimlers in Stalybridge Bus Station. Manchester 1357, an Ashton BUT, one of SHMD CVG6 71-76, SHMD CVD6 single-decker 104 and another SHMD Daimler in the background.
OTA/Reg Wilson

Carrying leather cash bag and 'Ultimate' ticket machine, the conductor of Ashton 87 chats to his driver as they await their departure time at Stalybridge. SHMD Northern Counties-bodied Daimler CVG6 83 is parked alongside.
Howard Piltz

Starting in January 1963, the 210 service was progressively changed to motor bus operation, the final trolleybuses running at the end of April. In this 1966 picture, 1342 passes a new Metro Cammell-bodied Daimler Fleetline working the 210x to Denton. The Fleetline is from the 4655-4684 batch. Below the Goodyear Tyres advertisement, the clock on the Transport Department's former head office is stopped and left set to mid-day, for 55 Piccadilly has also been abandoned, the Department having moved in 1963 to its new building in Devonshire Street North, adjacent to Hyde Road garage.
OTA/Reg Wilson

The 219 was converted without notice in October 1964. Delivery times for new buses were long in the 1960s and motor buses from other garages were moved to Hyde Road for the conversion. In this 1966 picture, the 219 is worked by 3328, a 1954 Northern Counties-bodied Leyland PD2 transferred from Parrs Wood, and by 3360, one of Hyde Road's 'own' Leyland-bodied Leyland PD2s new in 1953. 1948 Crossley DD42 2117 is working a 218x to Audenshaw. All three were older than the trolleybuses they replaced. The sole trolleybus is Ashton 86.
OTA/Reg Wilson

Continuing the old for new theme, on a dull day in 1965 Metro Cammell-bodied Leyland PD2 3216, new in 1951 and transferred from Queens Road garage, stands at the terminus in Ashton, the market in full swing. It is being passed by BUT 1311, bound for Stalybridge; in the background another Manchester BUT on the 218x picks its way through the crowds.
Howard Piltz

The Department's new headquarters building in Devonshire Street North was built on part of the Hyde Road garage site. BUT 1327 and another, en route to taking up service at Stevenson Square, are about to pass the new offices. A driver, in lightweight summer uniform jacket, waits to cross the road at the Hyde Road traffic lights.
Tony Belton

A section of the garage's main frontage on Hyde Road was also demolished to allow construction of new staff accommodation and a safer wide garage entrance to replace the narrow archways that dated back to tramway days. The old arch frames 1331. The folding doors beyond the bus are those of the former tower wagon garage, by then out of use.
Tony Belton

Above: Most dewirements were a simple matter of using the long bamboo pole, stored in a long tube beneath the body and pulled out from the back of the bus. The trolley boom springs were strong and if a trolley boom hit a span wire the results could be serious. At Ryecroft Hall, 1315's offside trolley boom has broken off at its springs and become entangled with the overhead wires; its other boom points skywards. Tower wagon A118 has arrived from Hyde Road and its crew, safely insulated, are dealing with the problem. Ashton 83 is passing, booms down and using its batteries, 1357 has already done this and its driver is waving 83 to overtake.
OTA/Reg Wilson

Below: Crews were always keen to avoid filling-in dewirement reports. In this incident at Guide Bridge, the bus turning on the 219x has dewired, its boom has bent and become caught on the span wire. The rules were that they should have phoned for the tower wagon, resulting in much form filling. To avoid this, the crew of the following 219 has stopped to help and whilst the 219x's driver inches forward on batteries, the other driver has climbed onto the roof (steps and grab rails were provided) to assist the guards pulling on the bamboo pole. All ended safely and successfully with both buses soon on their way and no paperwork.
OTA/Chris Bennett

The Final Evening

The last evening of public operation attracted a considerable number of people. Here Ashton 83 and 87 prepare to leave Portland Street on the 22.27hrs 218 to Stalybridge, Ashton's last departure from Manchester. The crowd, including enthusiasts' wives and girlfriends, spills over into the roadway.
Howard Piltz

From Stalybridge, Ashton 83 and 87 worked back to Ashton. 87's conductor pulls the Ashton Market 'frog' for the last time, setting the overhead for the final run to Mossley Road garage to bring Ashton's trolleybus operation to an end.
Tony Belton

The last public journey on the system was Manchester's 23.00hrs 215 from Stevenson Square to Audenshaw and back to Hyde Road garage on 30th December 1966. To ensure everyone got a seat, the Department provided an extra trolleybus, 1321 preceding 1354.
OTA/Reg Wilson

Midnight in Hyde Road Works' yard. The final pictures taken, the garage staff politely asked the enthusiasts to leave and got on with the next job.
OTA/Chris Bennett

On 31st December, the day after the final public journeys, Manchester generously gave two preserved vehicles, Manchester 1344 and Rotherham 44, the run of the Manchester sections of the system, leaving the power on and providing supervisory and operating staff. This picture nicely captures that 'morning after'. Below platforms 13 and 14 of Piccadilly station, Manchester's Leyland-bodied PD2 3360, new 1953, passes Rotherham 44 which is overtaking Ashton 53, one of eight Roe-bodied Leyland Atlanteans new in December for the conversion. All three show 218 on their indicators.
Tony Belton

The two preserved buses had to be tested by the Department's engineering staff, which they did the previous day with some amusement at the bewilderment of potential passengers when Rotherham 44 arrived in Ashton. 44 was a Daimler CTE6; originally a single-decker new in 1950, it was rebodied by Roe as a double-decker in 1957 and is now in the Trolleybus Museum at Sandtoft.
Howard Piltz

Good trolleybuses with years of life left in them. 1337 and six others along with much older withdrawn motor buses (ten Crossleys new in 1947/48 including 2006, 2014 and 2028, and Brush-bodied Daimlers 4058 and 4072) in the yard at Hyde Road works. All went for scrap.
Howard Piltz

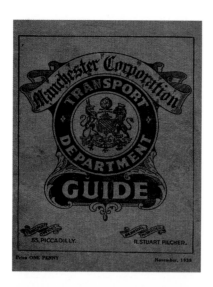
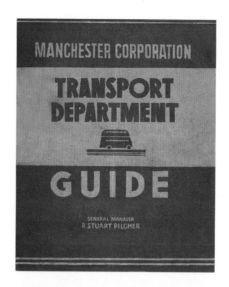

The covers of the Department's timetables varied over the years but, perhaps unsurprisingly, never featured a trolleybus.
These are for 1938, 1939, 1943, 1946, 1950,1960,1965 and 1966.
Authors' collection

There are few facts about whether SHMD ordered trolleybuses.

When conversion of the Hyde tram service 19 was agreed in 1939, it was stated that SHMD planned to share its trolleybus operation. On the other hand with an ever-decreasing number of its trams in good order, in 1935 SHMD had handed over to Manchester its duties on the 19 tram service.

Manchester ordered its vehicles for the Hyde trolleybus service in March 1939, planning delivery in about 8 months, and it seems reasonable that if SHMD was to participate it would have taken similar steps. There is no evidence of any such order in the SHMD minutes and records but a 1940 sales brochure produced by the Sunbeam Trolleybus Co Ltd of Wolverhampton listed SHMD as a customer. Manufacturers' sales brochures are sometimes not the most reliable documents but bus bodies and chassis were often started ahead of a formal order. Also, at the time there was something of a rush to obtain new buses in the face of the coming war.

Northern Counties of Wigan was SHMD's supplier of bodies and the two had a good relationship. The Wigan firm was owned by the Cardiff-based Lewis family, which had considerable industrial interests in that city. Northern Counties' registered office was there and it had supplied many of Cardiff Corporation's bus bodies. Cardiff decided to operate trolleybuses and in 1940 placed an order for its first — ten six-wheel Leylands. With the onset of war, the government cancelled them and substituted ten AEC 664T chassis intended for export — there were many such changes at the time.

The Cardiff vehicles, 201-210, arrived during 1941 and 1942, with Northern Counties bodies to prewar (not utility) standards. Research in Cardiff has produced an indication that these had been in build for SHMD and were redirected by the government, Northern Counties altering them to fit the AEC chassis.

Ten vehicles would be reasonable for SHMD's share of the Hyde service, although there has been conjecture that the number was six and that the six wartime Sunbeams delivered to Ashton were those originally

for SHMD, much rescheduled by the government.

Whether any SHMD vehicles would have been six- or four-wheelers is again a matter of guesswork. Manchester had ordered four-wheelers. If they were to have been four-wheelers, altering the bodies to add the extra bays to make them into six-wheelers for Cardiff was not difficult, as Northern Counties bodies had steel frames.

It seems possible that SHMD may have had some sort of informal agreements with Sunbeam and Northern Counties, hedging its bets against the uncertainty of war, and that with the decision to delay conversion of the Hyde service, the government reallocated the bodies and chassis assigned to SHMD. There is, however, no proof.

The Cardiff Transport Preservation Group provided a picture of one of the Cardiff vehicles and, using that and image processing software, here is a speculative picture of what an SHMD Northern Counties-bodied Sunbeam six-wheeler would have looked like waiting in Portland Street on the 210 in 1958.
Michael Eyre

This chapter was written for the original edition by the then Manchester Corporation Transport Department's Electrical Engineer, Fred Eversfield, MIEE; it has been updated where necessary by Geoff Burrows.

The first trolleybuses proved to be very reliable. Driven by former tramcar drivers, they suffered few dewirements and even newly trained staff found the vehicles easy to master. Controls were simple: the usual steering wheel, a handbrake and two pedals. The right pedal was the power control and the second pedal, on the left, operated the braking system. This differed from that of some earlier trolleybus systems, which used the opposite pedal arrangement. As the power pedal was depressed, it actuated magnetically operated switches ('contactors') which controlled the speed of the vehicle by gradually cutting out the starting resistances on the first few notches. Then further notches reduced the series and shunt field path of the current through the motor until full speed was reached. To facilitate training and ensure sufficient skilled drivers were available on opening day, the Department

built a trolleybus driving simulator, which was installed in the driving school at Hyde Road.

On the early vehicles regenerative braking was fitted. This effectively reversed the motor operation so that it became a dynamo, and generated power which it fed back into the overhead line for other vehicles to use. The effort in doing this slowed the vehicle smoothly, to about five miles per hour; below that the handbrake was used. For more severe braking further pressure on the pedal actuated the air operated drum brake system on the road wheels but this was rather too powerful for normal use. The postwar trolleybuses did not have regenerative braking, because the rotary generators, which converted the alternating current mains to the direct current line voltage, were being replaced by mercury arc (glass bulb) rectifiers that were less able to absorb the surges generated by braking. Instead they were equipped with rheostatic braking, which slowed the motor by loading it with the vehicle's control resistances. The dc line voltage was nominally 550volts, sometimes raised at the substation to

600volts to allow for voltage drop along the feeders.

A trolleybus chassis was not simply that of a motor bus with the engine removed and replaced by an electric motor. On a motor bus, the engine has a given capacity and the diesel fuel has a given calorific value so that there is a fixed maximum power output. Not so on a trolleybus, where the power output from an electric motor can be almost infinitely high for short periods, placing very high stresses on the transmission, rear axles and chassis frame. To give some idea of the load conditions that could occur, the main operating contactors had a continuous rating of 150 amps but a fully laden six-wheeler starting and accelerating up a steep gradient could draw 400 amps for a short period. The mechanical strength and electrical rating of the electrical equipment components therefore considerably exceeded the minimum requirements such that risk of damage from electrical overload was minimal almost up to short circuit conditions.

The postwar vehicles had automatic acceleration equipment, either when new

In Portland Street, 1162's trolley has dewired, broken the wooden spacer and become tangled with the span wire. Thornycroft A115's overhead line crew are putting things right. 1250, outbound for Denton on the 210x, creeps by on its batteries. In the distance, another six-wheeler is inbound on the 210x. 1122 loads for the Trough on the 218x.
Neville Knight

or fitted as a modification. This operated the contactor switching at a rate preset by the accelerating valve and gave very smooth acceleration,. The 1000- and 1100- series did not have automatic acceleration, the smoothness of the ride depending upon how carefully the driver operated the accelerator pedal. If he depressed this too quickly, going through the resistance notches on the controller and connecting the series field before the motor was able to accept the current, overload could occur. Protection was provided by circuit breakers, fitted on the cab roof above the driver's head, which would trip with a considerable thump.

Manchester trolleybuses had their control gear mounted in fireproof cabinets in the cab. The main motor resistances, which generated a fair amount of heat

Illuminated indicators were provided to show drivers which way the tongues of the turn-outs ('frogs') were set. The first picture is a manually operated turn-out at Ryecroft Hall, Audenshaw, with rope and wire pull. The second is the signal from the electrically operated unit at the junction of Piccadilly and Portland Street.
Robert Bonner, Chris Heaps

when in circuit, were suspended from the chassis frame, within the chassis on the 1000s, 1100s and 1300s and on outriggers at the side on the 1200s. At the top of the corner window pillar in front of the driver was a neon lamp, which remained lighted so long as there was power from the overhead and provided an indication if a trolley dewired.

A difficult problem for trolleybuses was fog. This required a driver to go slowly, using the resistance notches. Heat built up in the resistances and there could be insufficient air flow to cool them. If this continued for a long period there could be a risk of overheating. On some systems where attention was not paid to this, there were instances of dangerous vehicle fires but Manchester never had a serious problem in spite of the 'pea-soup' fogs in the years before smokeless zones.

Unlike many trolleybus systems, Manchester vehicles had batteries for manoeuvring away from the overhead. Either alkaline or lead-acid cells were used. The former had a long life of 15 years or more and could be charged and discharged quickly without damage but were expensive. The reliable lead-acid cells cost less and had a life of about five years but could not be charged so quickly. A fully charged set of batteries could drive a vehicle about half a mile, although with both types after manoeuvring some distance the battery voltage would drop. It would recover if left for a few minutes and would then be able to drive the vehicle for a further shorter distance.

On the 1000-, 1100- and 1200-series the batteries were charged from the line voltage by means of a motor-generator set, which consisted of a line voltage motor driving a low voltage dynamo. This provided current to charge the batteries, which also fed the vehicle lighting system — a very much bigger version, in fact, of the usual car battery and lighting system, except that the electric motor instead of the car engine drove the generator. On the 1300- series the generator was driven off the main traction motor shaft and charged when the vehicle was in motion.

Power was taken from the overhead line by two collector booms, made of steel tube wrapped with insulating tape and held against the overhead wire by strong springs. Contact was made with the line by a phosphor-bronze trolley head, fitted with a suitable carbon insert, which slid along the wire as the bus moved. The carbons wore as they slid and many types were tried to find that most suitable. The Edinburgh type was the longest (99.5mm) and heaviest grade, whilst the shortest and lightest were made by Ohio Brass. A length of 64mm was fairly general, but 72mm gave better service. The grade of carbon was important. Hard carbon lasted a long time

but wore the overhead wire, whilst soft carbon needed frequent changing on the road. Manchester found that a waterproof type was best in the damp climate.

Vehicles and overhead had to have regular tests for insulation to check whether any part was presenting a low impedance to earth. Vehicles were tested when in the garage; the overhead test could be done from substations even with vehicles in the section.

Electrical power was purchased from the Corporation Electricity Department and after nationalisation the North Western Electricity Board. Some operators generated their own power especially for the trolleybuses but Manchester did not. The substations were situated near to the trolleybus routes, and in these stations the alternating current supply was converted to the direct current supply for the overhead, by means of rotary converters or mercury arc rectifiers.

The electricity authority metered the direct current supply and thence the cables were fed to the 'street control box' — cast iron boxes set at the edge of the pavement — and up the 'traction pillar' — one of the overhead poles which was also used to carry the feeder cables to the overhead. Generally, traction pillars were situated about a mile apart and fed two sections, towards the city and away from the city, the end of each mile-long section having short insulated sections in the running wires. Sections were independently switched so that they could be isolated in case of fault. In some cases, each section was connected to the next by means of high-speed circuit breakers in the substation. In the city area where routes were more heavily loaded the feeders were at more frequent intervals along the route. Any short in the wiring would automatically trip the circuit breakers at the appropriate feeder.

A 500kilowatt substation would typically have in the region of 900 amps continuous output but would be capable of supplying double that for 15 seconds or thereabouts. Then a circuit breaker would trip out, automatically resetting after a few seconds. A persistent fault or continuous overload would trip and reset the breaker several times before staying out. A fault indicator would then be displayed at the substation and the distribution centre. Electricity supply was monitored by the Corporation Electricity Department (later the North Western Electricity Board) at their Dickinson Street Control Offices and the functioning of substation equipment could be checked directly therefrom.

In 1949 when the tramways were finally abandoned, and the tramway overhead was dismantled, the 'negative earth' connection (necessitated by the tram track being used as the negative 'wire') was removed from the trolleybus overhead and the system converted to 'all insulated' operation. Gradually all the old mechanical converters were replaced by mercury arc rectifiers and standardisation of track voltage established. Where track voltage had been standardised (made the same in all sections — a procedure not as simple as it sounds) the load on the various substations could be balanced by coupling sections together. Suitable precautions had to be taken and a device known as a 'Hastings Coupler' was used. This unit tripped the connection if the differential voltage between the coupled sections was more than ten volts, or if the current flow between the two sections was greater than the permitted normal value. Disconnection was maintained by the unit until conditions became normal again. Using Hastings Couplers, Manchester was able to couple Ashton Old and New Roads, from Pin Mill Brow to the Snipe, together with that section of overhead fed from the Great Ancoats Street substation.

The majority of the poles on trolleybus routes converted from tram routes dated back to the tramway era. However, as the trolleybus overhead was considerably heavier than the single tram wire, quite a number had to be replaced by heavier ones which were also required at junctions and curves.

Where one set of wiring crossed another, for example at turn-outs, insulated sections were inserted in the overhead. The trolleys passing over the junction run off the conductor wire on to an insulated runner, on to the metal junction or crossing, then across further insulation, and finally back on to the conductor wire again. Such junctions had to be negotiated with care. Drivers had to slow down and pass over the junctions with power off or severe arcing and burning of the running surface would take place. The speed and position of the vehicle have to be correct, to avoid dewiring the trolleys.

There were various types of turn-outs. Early ones were hand operated — the guard had to get off the bus and pull a rope handle at the end of a steel rod on an adjacent pole. This moved the tongues of the turn-out (points — 'frogs' in trolleybus parlance); he released the rope when the bus had crossed and then had to run and jump back onto his bus. Later types had to be pulled only to set them, as the trolleys

passed they caught a comb or wheel which tripped the tongues back to their normal state. The final development was automatic operation by the vehicle itself. The trolleys passed under a skate on the wires, about a vehicle's length before the turnout. This lifted the carbon off the conductor wire and, if the vehicle had power on, it drew its current through the skate, sending power through a solenoid which operated the tongues that switched the trolleys to the other line.

If power was not on when the trolley passed under the skate, then the solenoid did not operate and the frog remained set normally. After the vehicle had passed, the trolley head caught a skate or comb and reset the tongues. The setting of the frog on an automatic unit was indicated to the driver by a small box on an adjacent pole

that had illuminated slots to show which way it was set. Manual overrides were also provided.

On all turnouts, crossings, etc the speed of trolleybuses was limited to 5mph by the Ministry of Transport. The driver had to be careful and choose his pickup points to avoid arcing — bad driving would burn the insulated sections and shorten the life of the overhead. When planning the overhead careful thought had to be given to the suspension method — whether, for example, it should be from single traction pillars, with bracket arms (usually for single

track) or traction pillars on either side of the road, or even part traction pillar and part wall rosettes. The latter was a fixing bolted into the wall of a roadside building and required a legal agreement with the building's owner.

A typical Manchester suspension comprised, pole, pole strap, pole insulation, span wire (7/14 or 7/12 swg galvanised steel wire), pull-off, cap-and-cone line insulation, with wooden strain separator. Normally the negative line was nearest the kerb in the direction of travel. The conductor wire itself was cadmium copper 4/0 swg and cross-sectional area 0.125 inches, its cross section resembling that of a cottage loaf. Over the years various different proportions for the upper and lower lobe were used. Manchester originally specified the 'Portsmouth'

Guy tower wagon A120 on regular maintenance work replacing a feeder cable just east of Edge Lane, Droylsden on 12th June 1966. 1302's driver leans to the side of the cab to get clearance from the overhead crew. The power cables run down the 'traction pillar' on the right to feeder box 52.
Peter Thompson

section, which had rather a large radius of curvature for the top lobe. Later this upper radius was lessened and finally the Municipal Passenger Transport Association section was adopted. This latter had both the suspension and running lobes with the same radii. The groove in the cottage loaf section trolley wire was made when the wire was manufactured. Line ears (clamps) clipped into the groove and when tightened held it firmly without interfering with the running section of the wire. Manchester's wire was supplied in one mile lengths.

When running new trolley wire (or

taking it down for that matter) it was not simply a matter of running out the wire and fastening it up. It was necessary to pull up the slack, put tension on the wire, and for this suitable anchor points of sufficient strength had to be used, usually by anchoring back several strong poles, the one to the other, before the pull-up was commenced. Care was also required to ensure that the wire did not become twisted. Tension was then put on the wire with a pull-up tool, and the wire left to straighten and to stretch. The tension fell and the process was repeated, the ends finally being made off in the proper assemblies and the tension removed. Finally the line ears were fitted and tightened up, and the wire painted with graphite paint for smooth running. The life of the wire was about 15-20 years, depending upon the atmosphere, usage, failures, dewirements etc.

Careless driving of a trolleybus could cause a dewirement (trolleys coming off the wires) and this could damage the overhead, in the worst case bringing down live overhead wires. Vehicles were equipped with the usual bamboo pole to retrieve trolley booms. They were required to carry a pair of substantial rubber gloves to give insulation protection for the crew if necessary. Simple dewirements were dealt with by the driver and guard but for the more complex ones the crew would be expected to phone Central Control to summon an overhead line repair crew. Any dewirement had to be reported in some detail and these reports were regularly reviewed by the Department's engineers. As a result crews would make every effort to get the trolley booms back on the wire and continue their journey, thereby avoiding form filling and a possible managerial inquisition.

The overhead line crews were equipped with purpose-built vehicles known as 'tower wagons'. These had radio communication with Central Control and were fully equipped with all the tools and equipment necessary to deal with emergencies or faults. Manchester crews were responsible for erection of overhead besides maintenance. Their duties included attending to pillars damaged by cars and lorries running into them, high loads requiring escort, water bursts, fire calls, gas leaks etc., besides normal separator failures, wire breaks and so on. In winter overhead was treated with de-icing compounds to avoid freezing of points and frosting of wires. Trolley heads were also treated with de-icing fluid and in severe winter weather empty trolleybuses would be run throughout the night to keep the wires and points free of ice.

The roofs of the trolleybuses had duck boarding to allow fitters and linesmen to walk along the roof to attend to the trolley equipment. In order that crews or linesmen could work safely out of the rear emergency exit window or climb onto the roof, all Manchester trolleybuses carried a substantial steel and timber platform, stowed behind the rear-most upper-deck seat. This platform clipped onto the bottom edge of the emergency exit and was supported by chains which hooked onto the sides of the opening. It also had a folding step to facilitate climbing onto the roof. In spite of continual instructions from the garages, the platforms were rarely used, crews preferring the risky method of standing on the edge of the open emergency exit.

Manchester's Overhead Equipment Section also carried out equipment-proving tests for many other bodies and was involved with projects such as bridgeworks during the Manchester — London railway electrification project in the late 1950s.

MANCHESTER CORPORATION TRANSPORT DEPARTMENT

DEWIREMENT COMMITTEE

APPENDIX 'A'

SUMMARY OF REPORTED DEWIREMENTS FOR EIGHT WEEKS ENDED 21. 12. 1952

	HYDE ROAD GARAGE				ROCHDALE ROAD GARAGE			
	This period		Last period		This period		Last period	
	A.	B.	A.	B.	A.	B.	A.	B.
W. (wide driving)	5	–	8	–	9	–	23	–
S. (excessive speed)...	32	–	26	–	40	–	35	–
V. (defective vehicle).	–	3	–	11	–	6	–	8
O. (defective O.E.)....	–	3	–	3	–	5	–	3
F. (incorrect switch operation-Driver)..	1	–	5	–	3	–	7	–
Fx.(incorrect switch operation-Conductor)	4	–	1	–	3	–	2	–
M. (miscellaneous)	1	5	3	3	3	6	1	2
U. (unknown)	–	1	–	2	–	3	–	2
Totals	43	12	43	19	58	22	68	15

	Hyde Road Garage	Rochdale Road Garage
Number of buses in service	65	100

A = Dewirements classified as avoidable.

B = Dewirements classified as unavoidable

FLEET MILEAGE

Hyde Road Garage	352,509	1.56	dewirements per 10,000 miles
(Last period)		1.76	" " " "
Rochdale Road Garage	568,616	1.40	" " " "
(Last period)		1.46	" " " "

Total reported dewirements	:	135
Total fleet mileages	:	921,125
Dewirements per 10,000 miles	:	1.57

The Department took dewirements seriously and the Dewirement Committee met every eight weeks to review them and take any necessary action. The most frequent cause was excessive speed at junctions.
MCT via Keith Walker

Driving simulators are familiar things in 2007 but in 1938 they were unusual and advanced. This is the trolleybus driving simulator which the Department built and installed in its Hyde Road driving school. It showed the trainee a circuit diagram, the relevant parts of which lit up as he pressed the pedals. Below was a working set of contactor gear which the trainee could observe operating.
Omnibus Society Library/Ted Jones

Right: To supplement the purpose-built Thornycrofts, in 1945 the Department converted petrol-engined 1930 Leyland Tiger 109 to tower wagon A117, in which guise it served until the end of 1958. An interesting conversion with the tower emerging through a hole in the roof of the bus body, which was cut off behind the rear wheels. Infrequently used for overhead work, its main duty was tree lopping.
MCT/Michael Eyre

Below: The London — Manchester railway electrification project involved new bridges over Hyde Road and Fairfield Road. The work was carried out with a minimum of interruption to the trolleybuses, the overhead line crews fitting special wiring and protective covers, as here at Fairfield Street in June 1959. 1314 passes slowly under the temporary steel structure.
Peter Caunt

With the benefit of hindsight it is easy to see that two factors and no others ensured that Manchester's trolleybus network would not develop, and that the reasons advanced from time to time were really only secondary.

First was the police refusal to allow trolleybuses on Market Street and Deansgate — and consequently nearly all the other major shopping and business thoroughfares of the city. This effectively deprived the trolleybuses of the rich traffic generated in these areas, making them deposit their passengers on the fringe of the city centre. Even in Piccadilly they were mainly banished to the end furthest from the busiest area.

Second was the lack of interest in trolleybuses shown by almost all the joint operators. Joint operation was a cornerstone of the city's bus operations; had other operators been more trolleybus-minded then the wires might have gone up in Market Street and elsewhere. As it was, cross-city trolleybus services with all their advantages and extra revenue were impossible and passengers living in the trolleybus-served suburbs were denied this facility.

Just how important this was is shown by the new and replacement services. After the trolleybuses had gone, Rochdale Road had the 112/113 to Sale, also in Moston the 80 cross-city to Chorlton was reinstated and,

very soon after, its planned prewar extension along Charlestown Road was introduced with alternate buses as service 88. On Ashton New Road since 1946 the 83 service had run every 15 minutes across the city to Old Trafford and Firswood. Hyde Road had been served by the 57/77 to Salford and Swinton/Pendlebury from 1951. Ashton Old Road was to benefit from a cross-city service that was almost a reincarnation of prewar 15 service when, a few years later, the SELNEC PTE linked the 219 to former Salford services 64/66 to give a service from Ashton across the two cities to Eccles and Peel Green.

Stuart Pilcher would indeed have smiled once again.

Cross-city links were important revenue earners and were introduced, paralleling the trolleybuses, or restored when the trolleybuses were abandoned. Princess Road garage's Daimler CVG6 4135 on Rochdale Road on the 112 to Sale; similar 4107 on the 80 to Chorlton; Hyde Road's Leyland PD2/12 3369 on the 83 to Firswood; Salford Daimler CVG6 351 turning into Piccadilly Bus Station on the 77 from Reddish to Pendlebury and, in 1972, SELNEC 3137 (formerly Salford 291) at London Road Fire Station en route to Ashton from Peel Green on the 64/66.
Ray Dunning/Ray Dunning/Peter Thompson/Reg Wilson/Peter Thompson

Manchester

Format of the lists, from left to right: fleet number, maker's chassis number, date vehicle delivered (many were stored for extended periods), date vehicle entered public service, date vehicle last ran in service (withdrawn trolleybuses were often retained in reserve or for spares for as long as two years before final disposal), code showing to whom the vehicle was sold:

A	Aluminium & Allied Products, scrap dealers, Dukinfield		R	R. Charlton & Sons, scrap dealers, Bolton
B	R. Blair, scrap dealers, Manchester (some via J. Glynn, a Blair nominee)		S	R. Salmon, scrap dealers, Manchester
			T	Thompson, scrap dealers, Bury
C	S. J. & R. Cubbins, scrap dealers, Farnworth, Bolton		U	Autospares Ltd, scrap dealers, Bingley
D	H. J. Davies, scrap dealers, Worsley		V	Chassis scrapped after accident, body to Jenkinson, scrap dealer, Ashton-under-Lyne
H	Springhead Stone Co Ltd, scrap dealers, Oldham			
J	Jackson Bros, scrap dealers, Bradford		W	Thos. W. Ward Ltd, scrap dealers, Sheffield
K	Cut up by MCT at Hyde Road yard		X	Hardwick & Jones, scrap dealers, Carlton, Barnsley
M	Milleon Partners, scrap dealers, Barnsley		Y	Maudland Metals, scrap dealers, Preston
N	North's (P.V.) Ltd, dealer, Leeds		Z	Askin, scrap dealers, Barnsley
P	Sold to enthusiasts for preservation			

Precise days are shown where of interest and if available from the department's engineering records. Some dates and details are corrected from the previous edition of this book and "The Manchester Bus".

The Department allocated a "type number" to each batch or model. The code was not carried on the vehicle. Trolleybus types commenced at 90, away from the bus series then at about 30.

1000-1027   **DXJ 951-978**

Chassis	Crossley TDD4
Motor	Metropolitan Vickers MV202FW, compound-wound, 85hp at 550 volts
Control gear	Regenerative
Body	Metro Cammell-Crossley H28/26R Streamline
Trim	Lower saloon green moquette, later retrimmed in red; upper saloon red leather
MCT Type	90
Unladen weight	7tons 9cwt 3qrs
Allocation	All new to Rochdale Road; 1024-27 to Hyde Road 6/52 and back to Rochdale Road 1/55
	1001/04-06 (8/55), 1015/18/19/21-23/27 (10/55) to Hyde Road with the progressive closure of Rochdale Road

1000	92402	5/12/37	1/1/38	7/55	N		1010	92412	2/5/38	6/5/38	2/55	T		1020	92422	20/5/38	1/8/38	4/55	S
1001	92403	5/12/37	1/2/38	11/55	N		1011	92413	19/5/38	1/6/38	7/55	N		1021	92423	4/3/38	1/8/38	9/55	N
1002	92404	5/12/37	1/3/38	7/55	N		1012	92414	16/5/38	1/8/38	7/55	S		1022	92424	3/6/38	1/8/38	12/55	N
1003	92405	5/12/37	1/3/38	10/54	T		1013	92415	5/4/38	1/8/38	7/55	N		1023	92425	11/5/38	1/8/38	1/56	N
1004	92406	5/12/37	1/3/38	11/55	N		1014	92416	31/5/38	1/8/38	7/55	N		1024	92426	13/5/38	1/8/38	1/56	N
1005	92407	5/12/37	1/3/38	12/55	N		1015	92417	7/5/38	1/8/38	1/56	N		1025	92427	10/5/38	1/8/38	1/56	N
1006	92408	5/12/37	1/3/38	1/56	N		1016	92418	2/5/38	6/5/38	3/53	A		1026	92428	28/5/38	1/8/38	1/56	N
1007	92409	5/12/37	1/3/38	7/55	N		1017	92419	25/5/38	1/8/38	9/54	S		1027	92429	17/5/38	1/8/38	1/56	N
1008	92410	15/2/38	1/3/38	11/55	N		1018	92420	2/6/38	1/8/38	1/56	N							
1009	92411	11/1/38	1/3/38	1/56	N		1019	92421	8/5/38	1/8/38	1/56	N							

1028-1037   **DXJ 979-988**

Chassis	Leyland TB6
Motor	Metropolitan Vickers MV202FW, compound-wound, 85hp at 550 volts
Control gear	Regenerative
Body	Metro Cammell-Crossley H28/26R Streamline
Trim	Lower saloon green moquette, later retrimmed in red; upper saloon red leather
MCT Type	92
Unladen weight	7tons 9cwt 1 or 2qrs
Allocation	All always at Rochdale Road

1028	13611	18/3/38	25/3/38	11/55	N		1033	13616	23/3/38	25/3/38	11/51	A		*1033/35 retained in store until 1955.*
1029	13612	18/3/38	25/3/38	6/54	A		1034	13617	24/3/38	25/3/38	11/55	N		
1030	13613	18/3/38	25/3/38	5/55	A		1035	13618	24/3/38	25/3/38	12/51	A		
1031	13614	18/3/38	25/3/38	9/54	A		1036	13619	24/3/38	25/3/38	11/54	A		
1032	13615	23/3/38	25/3/38	5/55	A		1037	13620	23/3/38	25/3/38	10/54	A		

1050-1061   **DXJ 989-993, ENB 175-181**

Chassis	Crossley TDD6
Motor	Metropolitan Vickers MV206A2, compound-wound, 95hp at 550 volts
Control gear	Regenerative
Body	Metro Cammell-Crossley H38/30R Streamline
Trim	Lower saloon green moquette, later retrimmed in red; upper saloon red leather
MCT Type	91
Unladen weight	9tons 2cwt 0 or 1qrs
Allocation	All new to Rochdale Road, 1050/2/4/7/8 to Hyde Road 4/56 with the progressive closure of Rochdale Road

1050	92302	13/3/38	14/3/38	4/56	B	1056	92308	6/3/38	7/3/38	2/51	D	
1051	92303	15/2/38	1/3/38	2/51	D	1057	92309	6/3/38	7/3/38	4/56	C	
1052	92304	15/2/38	1/3/38	4/56	C	1058	92310	6/3/38	7/3/38	4/56	C	
1053	92305	6/3/38	7/3/38	11/55	N	1059	92311	10/3/38	11/3/38	9/51	A	
1054	92306	6/3/38	7/3/38	4/56	C	1060	92312	13/3/38	14/3/38	3/56	C	
1055	92307	6/3/38	7/3/38	8/50	D	1061	92313	10/3/38	11/3/38	7/50	K	

1051/55/56/59/61 retained in store or used for spares; 1051/55/56 sold 1953; 1059 sold 1955; 1061 cutup 1953

1062-1087   **ENB 182-207**

Chassis	Leyland TTB4
Motor	1062-1072: Metropolitan Vickers 206A2, compound-wound, 95hp at 550 volts
	1073-1087: Metropolitan Vickers 206A5, compound-wound, 95hp at 550 volts
Control gear	Regenerative
Body	Metro Cammell-Crossley H38/30R Streamline
Trim	Lower saloon green moquette, later retrimmed in red; upper saloon red leather
Type	93
Unladen weight	9tons 1 or 2cwt 0 qrs
Allocation	All new to Rochdale Road, 1062-1071 to Hyde Road 7/41
	1070/1 to Rochdale Road 4/46, 1070 to Hyde Road 1/48 and to Rochdale Road 9/48
	1062 (10/51), 1063/65 (7/51), 1068/69 (3/51) to Rochdale Road
	1074/79 to Hyde Road 4/56 with the progressive closure of Rochdale Road

1062	13600	-/1/38	1/3/38	3/56	N	1073	15885	-/4/38	1/8/38	8/50	D	1084	15896	-/6/38	1/8/38	1/55	A	
1063	13601	-/1/38	1/3/38	1/56	N	1074	15886	-/4/38	1/8/38	4/56	C	1085	15897	-/6/38	1/8/38	11/50	D	
1064	13602	-/1/38	1/3/38	8/50	D	1075	15887	-/4/38	1/8/38	5/55	A	1086	15898	-/6/38	1/8/38	11/50	D	
1065	13603	-/2/38	1/3/38	11/54	A	1076	15888	-/5/38	1/8/38	1/53	H	1087	15899	-/6/38	1/8/38	12/55	N	
1066	13604	-/2/38	1/3/38	8/50	D	1077	15889	-/5/38	1/8/38	9/51	A							
1067	13605	-/2/38	1/3/38	5/51	D	1078	15890	-/5/38	1/8/38	9/50	D	*1064/66/67/71/73/77/78/80/81/82/83/85/86*						
1068	13606	-/2/38	1/3/38	4/55	A	1079	15891	-/5/38	1/8/38	4/56	C	*retained in store or used for spares;*						
1069	13607	-/2/38	1/3/38	11/55	N	1080	15892	-/6/38	1/8/38	9/50	D	*1064/67/73/78/80/83/85/86 sold 1953;*						
1070	13608	-/2/38	1/3/38	4/55	A	1081	15893	-/6/38	1/8/38	6/51	A	*1071/77/81 sold 1955; 1066/82 cut up 1953*						
1071	13609	-/2/38	9/2/38	6/51	A	1082	15894	-/6/38	1/8/38	6/50	K							
1072	13610	-/2/38	1/3/38	2/52	A	1083	15895	-/6/38	1/8/38	4/51	D							

1100-1136   **GNA 18-54**

Chassis	Leyland TB5
Motor	Metropolitan Vickers 202FW, compound-wound, 85hp at 550 volts
Control gear	Regenerative
Body	English Electric H28/26R Streamline —
	upgraded type with deeper seats, double-skin roof and reduced rear and side indicators.
Trim	Lower saloon red moquette; upper saloon red leather
MCT Type	92
Unladen weight	7tons 9cwt 2qrs
Notes	1104 had an early form of automatic acceleration control equipment when new. 1104 and 1105 had six (as opposed to three) lines of text on the intermediate blind. The English Electric body differed from the Crossley body in many details, including the front grille and the position of the headlamps and trafficators. The bodies carried no indication of their maker.
Allocation	All new to Rochdale Road, 1104 (3/56), 1109 (4/56) and 1133 (4/56) to Hyde Road with the progressive closure of Rochdale Road
Livery	None received the 'all red' livery

1100	303431	21/3/40	5/4/40	11/55	N	1113	303444	10/4/40	14/7/41	11/55	N	1126	303457	27/4/40	1/9/40	3/56	C	
1101	303432	29/3/40	1/11/40	2/55	N	1114	303445	17/4/40	1/11/40	12/55	N	1127	303458	30/4/40	14/7/41	3/56	C	
1102	303433	4/4/40	1/11/40	1/56	N	1115	303446	27/4/40	1/9/40	1/56	N	1128	303459	6/5/40	14/7/41	7/55	N	
1103	303434	29/3/40	1/11/40	1/56	N	1116	303447	18/4/40	14/7/41	1/56	N	1129	303460	22/4/40	1/11/40	7/54	A	
1104	303435	29/3/40	1/11/40	1/59	B	1117	303448	11/4/40	14/7/41	1/56	N	1130	303461	29/4/40	1/9/40	6/54	A	
1105	303436	5/4/40	1/11/40	11/54	A	1118	303449	30/3/40	5/4/40	2/55	A	1131	303462	5/4/40	1/9/40	2/56	N	
1106	303437	30/3/40	1/11/40	6/55	N	1119	303450	13/5/40	1/11/40	9/54	A	1132	303463	19/4/40	1/11/40	2/56	N	
1107	303438	5/4/40	1/11/40	8/55	A	1120	303451	13/4/40	14/7/41	2/55	A	1133	303464	30/5/40	1/11/40	1/59	B	
1108	303439	17/4/40	1/11/40	11/55	N	1121	303452	4/5/40	1/8/41	1/56	N	1134	303465	1/5/40	14/7/41	1/56	N	
1109	303440	6/4/40	14/7/41	4/56	C	1122	303453	14/5/40	1/11/40	7/55	N	1135	303466	29/5/40	1/11/40	6/55	N	
1110	303441	11/4/40	1/7/40	11/55	N	1123	303454	4/5/40	14/7/41	6/55	A	1136	303467	6/6/40	1/9/40	9/55	N	
1111	303442	12/4/40	1/11/40	11/55	N	1124	303455	6/6/40	1/9/40	2/55	A							
1112	303443	20/4/40	1/11/40	1/56	N	1125	303456	29/3/40	5/4/40	2/56	N							

1137-1176 GNA 55-94

Chassis	Crossley TDD4
Motor	Metropolitan Vickers 202FW, compound-wound, 85hp at 550 volts
Control gear	Regenerative
Body	Metro Cammell-Crossley H28/26R Streamline upgraded type
Trim	Lower saloon red moquette; upper saloon red leather
MCT Type	90
Unladen weight:	7tons 9cwt 0qrs
Allocation	1137/38, 1163-1176 new to Rochdale Road, 1139-1162 new to Hyde Road
	1139-1142 (9/50), 1143 (10/51), 1144-1148 (6/52) to Rochdale Road; 1145-1148 to Hyde Road 3/53
	1137/41/43/44/63/64 (4/55), 1141 (7/55), 1165-1169/74 (10/55), 1170-72/75 (1/56), 1173/76 (4/56)
	to Hyde Road with the progressive closure of Rochdale Road
Livery	None received the 'all red' livery

No	Batch				Code
1137	92450	9/2/40	9/2/40	7/55	N
1138	92452	1/2/40	2/2/40	10/54	S
1139	92453	12/2/40	1/3/40	8/53	W
1140	92451	20/2/40	1/3/40	7/55	N
1141	92454	23/2/40	1/3/40	8/55	N
1142	92455	20/3/40	5/4/40	1/56	N
1143	92456	3/4/40	5/4/40	1/56	N
1144	92457	20/3/40	5/4/40	7/55	N
1145	92458	28/3/40	5/4/40	7/55	N
1146	92459	2/4/40	5/4/40	2/56	N
1147	92461	9/4/40	14/7/41	5/59	B
1148	92462	11/4/40	14/7/41	5/59	B
1149	92460	17/4/40	14/7/41	2/56	N
1150	92463	19/4/40	14/7/41	5/59	B
1151	92464	2/5/40	4/7/41	5/59	B
1152	92465	4/5/40	14/7/41	5/59	B
1153	92466	15/5/40	14/7/41	4/59	B
1154	92467	1/6/40	1/7/40	1/56	N
1155	92469	29/5/40	1/9/40	12/55	N
1156	92468	5/6/40	14/7/41	1/59	B
1157	92470	12/6/40	1/9/40	2/56	N
1158	92471	16/6/40	1/7/40	10/58	B
1159	92472	21/6/40	14/7/41	3/59	B
1160	92473	15/7/40	1/9/40	1/55	S
1161	92474	31/7/40	1/9/40	3/59	B
1162	92475	30/8/40	1/11/40	5/59	B
1163	92476	31/10/40	14/7/41	6/59	B
1164	92477	21/11/40	19/12/40	11/59	B
1165	92478	25/11/40	19/12/40	8/60	B
1166	92479	6/12/40	19/12/40	9/60	B
1167	92480	30/1/41	14/7/41	5/59	B
1168	92481	10/3/41	14/7/41	5/59	B
1169	92482	19/4/41	14/7/41	3/60	B
1170	92483	25/6/41	14/7/41	8/60	B
1171	92484	3/8/41	3/8/41	5/59	B
1172	92485	12/11/41	1/2/42	1/59	B
1173	92486	30/1/42	1/3/42	1/59	B
1174	92487	14/10/42	1/11/42	6/60	B
1175	92488	9/7/43	1/9/43	5/59	B
1176	92489	13/3/43	25/3/43	5/59	B

1200-1237 JVU 707-744

Chassis	Crossley Empire TDD42/1
Motor	Metropolitan Vickers MV209AY1, compound-wound, 95hp at 550 volts
Control gear	Non-regenerative, stabilised rheostatic control
Body	Crossley H32/26R 8ft wide
Trim	Lower saloon red moquette; upper saloon red leather
MCT Type	94
Unladen weight	8tons 13cwt 3qrs
Notes	Apart from those for Ashton and two chassis for Cleethorpes these were the only vehicles of their type. Around 1952 modifications were made to overcome their very heavy steering
Modification	Automatic acceleration control equipment was fitted to 1201 and 1204 when new; the rest were retrospectively fitted with this equipment in 1950 or 1952: 6/50:1225-30/32/34/35; 7/50:1213/31/33/36/37; 8/50:1207/11/15; 9/50:1205/08/09/21; 10/50:1210/12/17/18; 11/50:1206; 3/52: 1200/02/03/14/16/19/20/22/23/24
Allocation	Hyde Road
Livery	Only 1203 received the 'all red' livery

No	Batch				Code
1200	94405	25/4/49	25/4/49	6/63	R
1201	94406	14/4/49	19/4/49	4/63	J
1202	94422	13/5/49	13/5/49	6/63	R
1203	94421	20/5/49	1/6/49	1/63	R
1204	94404	25/4/49	2/5/49	6/63	J
1205	94402	9/5/49	9/5/49	5/63	B
1206	94403	2/5/49	3/5/49	6/63	R
1207	94411	26/5/49	1/6/49	4/63	B
1208	94408	1/6/49	1/6/49	4/63	B
1209	94407	8/6/49	8/6/49	5/63	B
1210	94419	30/6/49	1/7/49	1/63	R
1211	94420	14/6/59	14/6/49	4/63	B
1212	94409	1/7/49	1/7/49	4/63	B
1213	94413	1/7/49	1/7/49	1/63	R
1214	94418	6/7/49	7/7/49	7/63	J
1215	94410	8/7/49	11/7/49	1/63	R
1216	94414	6/7/49	6/7/49	4/63	B
1217	94415	6/7/49	6/7/49	7/63	J
1218	94412	22/7/49	13/10/49	1/63	R
1219	94425	12/8/49	13/10/49	1/63	R
1220	94426	2/9/49	1/1/50	4/63	B
1221	94423	12/8/49	1/1/50	4/63	B
1222	94424	26/8/49	1/1/50	7/63	J
1223	94417	15/8/49	1/1/50	4/63	B
1224	94428	2/9/49	1/1/50	4/63	B
1225	94416	31/8/49	1/1/50	7/63	J
1226	94427	30/9/49	1/1/50	7/63	J
1227	94401	30/9/49	*1/1/50	4/63	B
1228	94430	4/10/49	1/1/50	10/63	M
1229	94431	4/10/49	1/1/50	1/63	R
1230	94429	19/10/49	1/1/50	10/63	M
1231	94433	7/10/49	1/1/50	4/63	B
1232	94432	7/10/49	1/1/50	10/63	M
1233	94434	19/10/49	1/1/50	1/63	R
1234	94436	20/10/49	1/1/50	10/63	M
1235	94435	14/10/49	1/1/50	10/63	M
1236	94437	26/10/49	1/1/50	1/63	R
1237	94438	28/10/49	1/1/50	7/63	J

*1227 used 9/49 for 210 route testing

1240-1255   JVU 745-760

Chassis	Crossley Dominion 3-axle TDD64/1
Motor	Metropolitan Vickers MV210AY1, compound-wound, 115hp at 550 volts
Control gear	Non-regenerative, stabilised rheostatic control, automatic acceleration from new
Body	Crossley H36/30R 8ft wide
Trim	Lower saloon red moquette; upper saloon red leather
MCT Type	95
Unladen weight	10tons 3cwt 2qrs
Allocation	Hyde Road
Notes	Even heavier steering than 1200-1237, modifications to lighten steering fitted from 1952. 1240-1255 were the only examples of the TDD64 built
Livery	None received the 'all red' livery

1240	94503	16/1/51	1/3/51	7/63	J	1248	94510	2/2/51	1/3/51	6/63	J
1241	94507	26/1/51	1/3/51	7/63	J	1249	94511	5/2/51	1/3/51	7/63	J
1242	94504	26/1/51	1/3/51	4/63	B	1250	94512	6/2/51	1/3/51	7/63	P
1243	94502	27/1/51	1/3/51	1/63	R	1251	94506	7/2/51	1/3/51	1/63	R
1244	94505	30/1/51	1/3/51	1/63	R	1252	94514	26/2/51	1/10/51	1/63	R
1245	94509	31/1/51	1/3/51	1/63	R	1253	94513	15/3/51	1/9/51	4/63	B
1246	94508	2/2/51	1/3/51	7/63	J	1254	94515	26/2/51	1/9/51	7/63	J
1247	94501	5/2/51	1/3/51	1/63	R	1255	94516	22/3/51	1/10/51	4/63	B

1301-1362   ONE 701-762

Chassis	British United Traction Ltd ('BUT') 9612T
Motor	Metropolitan Vickers MV209AYG10, compound-wound, 95hp at 550 volts
Control gear	Non-regenerative, stabilised rheostatic control, automatic acceleration
Body	Burlingham H32/28R 8ft wide, 27ft long, body numbers 5648-5709
Trim	Lower saloon green moquette; upper saloon brown leathercloth
MCT Type	96
Unladen weight	8tons 8cwt 2qrs
Allocation	When new 1301-20, 1331-40, 1351-62 were at Rochdale Road and 1321-1330, 1341-1350 were at Hyde Road. All moved to Hyde Road as Rochdale Road closed
Livery	1312/38/9/40/6/7 were never repainted into the 'all red' livery

1301	9612T.185	11/8/55	1/9/55	12/66	X	1332	9612T.216	4/11/55	1/12/55	11/66	Y
1302	9612T.186	2/6/55	13/6/55	12/66	Y	1333	9612T.217	5/11/55	1/12/55	12/66	Y
1303	9612T.187	12/8/55	1/9/55	10/66	B	1334	9612T.218	8/11/55	1/12/55	12/66	Y
1304	9612T.188	26/8/55	1/9/55	12/66	X	1335	9612T.219	10/11/55	1/12/55	12/64	U
1305	9612T.189	8/9/55	1/10/55	12/64	U	1336	9612T.220	12/11/55	1/12/55	12/66	Y
1306	9612T.190	16/9/55	1/10/55	12/66	B	1337	9612T.221	14/11/55	1/12/55	12/64	U
1307	9612T.191	24/9/55	1/10/55	12/64	U	1338	9612T.222	17/11/55	1/12/55	12/64	U
1308	9612T.192	22/9/55	1/10/55	12/66	Y	1339	9612T.223	18/11/55	1/12/55	12/64	U
1309	9612T.193	27/9/55	1/10/55	12/64	U	1340	9612T.224	15/11/55	1/12/55	12/64	U
1310	9612T.194	28/9/55	1/10/55	12/64	U	1341	9612T.225	21/11/55	1/12/55	12/66	Y
1311	9612T.195	29/9/55	1/10/55	12/64	U	1342	9612T.226	22/11/55	1/12/55	10/66	B
1312	9612T.196	3/10/55	6/10/55	11/63	U	1343	9612T.227	23/11/55	1/12/55	2/66	U
1313	9612T.197	4/10/55	6/10/55	2/66	U	1344	9612T.228	24/11/55	1/12/55	7/64	P
1314	9612T.198	1/10/55	13/10/55	12/66	Y	1345	9612T.229	25/11/55	1/12/55	12/64	U
1315	9612T.199	5/10/55	24/10/55	12/66	Y	1346	9612T.230	6/12/55	6/12/55	1/62	V
1316	9612T.200	7/10/55	24/10/55	12/64	U	1347	9612T.231	27/11/55	1/12/55	12/64	U
1317	9612T.201	8/10/55	1/11/55	7/64	Z	1348	9612T.232	8/12/55	1/1/56	2/66	U
1318	9612T.202	10/10/55	1/11/55	12/66	Y	1349	9612T.233	7/12/55	1/1/56	6/66	B
1319	9612T.203	13/10/55	1/11/55	12/64	U	1350	9612T.234	9/12/55	1/1/56	12/66	Y
1320	9612T.204	12/10/55	1/11/55	10/66	B	1351	9612T.235	14/12/55	1/1/56	12/64	U
1321	9612T.205	13/10/55	18/10/55	12/66	Y	1352	9612T.236	5/1/56	1/2/56	2/66	U
1322	9612T.206	18/10/55	24/10/55	12/66	Y	1353	9612T.237	16/1/56	1/1/56	6/66	B
1323	9612T.207	19/10/55	24/10/55	12/64	U	1354	9612T.238	4/1/56	1/2/56	12/66	Y
1324	9612T.208	20/10/55	1/11/55	8/66	X	1355	9612T.239	9/1/56	1/2/56	12/64	U
1325	9612T.209	22/10/55	1/11/55	12/66	Y	1356	9612T.240	11/1/56	1/2/56	12/66	Y
1326	9612T.210	25/10/55	1/11/55	12/64	U	1357	9612T.241	13/1/56	1/2/56	12/66	Y
1327	9612T.211	28/10/55	1/11/55	12/64	U	1358	9612T.242	16/1/56	1/2/56	12/64	U
1328	9612T.212	31/10/55	1/11/55	6/66	Y	1359	9612T.243	17/1/56	1/2/56	12/66	Y
1329	9612T.213	29/10/55	1/11/55	12/66	Y	1360	9612T.244	26/1/56	1/2/56	4/64	U
1330	9612T.214	2/11/55	1/12/55	12/66	X	1361	9612T.245	22/2/56	1/3/56	12/64	U
1331	9612T.215	3/11/55	1/12/55	12/64	U	1362	9612T.246	6/3/56	25/3/56	12/66	Y

Ashton-under-Lyne

This book is concerned with the modern trolleybus system. However for the sake of completeness, brief details of the early Ashton trolleybuses are shown. List format, from left to right: fleet number, registration number, chassis make and type, motor make and type (MV = Metropolitan Vickers, EE = English Electric), chassis number, make of body, seating capacity, date vehicle first entered public service, date vehicle last ran in service, code showing to whom the vehicle was sold, as follows:

F Bradford Corporation, allocated fleet numbers 801, 800 but not used; sold to Autospares Ltd, Bingley, for scrap 1962
L T. Marler & Sons Ltd, Dukinfield, scrap dealers
N North's (P.V.) Ltd, dealer, Leeds
P Preserved
U Autospares Ltd, scrap dealers, Bingley
S sold for scrap

50	TD 2362	Railless LFT30	2 x EEC 99A 35hp	-	Short	B36C	8/25	2/39	S	Note H
51	TD 2497	Railless LFT30	2 x EEC 99A 35hp	-	Short	B36C	8/25	2/39	S	Note H
52	TD 3147	Railless LFT30	2 x EEC 99A 35hp	-	Short	B36C	8/25	-/37	S	Note H
53	TD 3148	Railless LFT30	2 x EEC 99A 35hp	-	Short	B36C	8/25	2/39	S	Note H
54	TD 3207	Railless LFT30	2 x EEC 99A 35hp	-	Short	B36C	8/25	2/39	S	Note H
55	TD 3208	Railless LFT30	2 x EEC 99A 35hp	-	Short	B36C	8/25	-/37	S	Note H
56	TD 3262	Railless LFT30	2 x EEC 99A 35hp	-	Short	B36C	8/25	2/39	S	Note H
57	TD 3344	Railless LFT30	2 x EEC 99A 35hp	-	Short	B36C	8/25	2/39	S	Note H
48	CTD 547	Leyland TB4	MV202FW 85hp	14194	Eng Electric	H30/26R	11/37	10/56	N	Note A
52	CTD 548	Leyland TB4	MV202FW 85hp	14195	Eng Electric	H30/26R	11/37	9/56	N	Note A
55	CTD 549	Leyland TB4	MV202FW 85hp	14196	Eng Electric	H30/26R	11/37	9/56	N	Note A
49	CTD 787	Crossley TDD4	MV202 82hp	92401	MC-Crossley	H28/26R	12/37	10/56	N	Note A, B
46	CTF 313	Crossley TDD6	MV206A2 95hp	92314	MC-Crossley	H38/26R	3/38	10/51	L	
47	CTF 314	Crossley TDD6	MV206A2 95hp	92315	MC-Crossley	H38/30R	3/38	10/51	L	
58	CNE 474	Crossley TDD6	MV206A2 95hp	92301	MC-Crossley	H38/30R	6/38	1/55	N	Note C
50	ETE 811	Crossley TDD4	MV202FW 85hp	92490	MC-Crossley	H28/26R	2/40	10/56	N	
51	ETE 812	Crossley TDD4	MV202FW 85hp	92491	MC-Crossley	H28/26R	2/40	8/60	N	
53	ETE 813	Crossley TDD4	MV202FW 85hp	92492	MC-Crossley	H28/26R	2/40	10/56	N	
54	ETE 814	Crossley TDD4	MV202FW 85hp	92493	MC-Crossley	H28/26R	5/40	8/60	N	
56	ETE 815	Crossley TDD4	MV202FW 85hp	92494	MC-Crossley	H28/26R	5/40	9/56	N	
57	ETE 816	Crossley TDD4	MV202FW 85hp	92495	MC-Crossley	H28/26R	5/40	10/54	N	
59	ETE 817	Crossley TDD4	MV202FW 85hp	92496	MC-Crossley	H28/26R	5/40	10/54	N	
60	ETE 818	Crossley TDD4	MV202FW 85hp	92497	MC-Crossley	H28/26R	7/40	10/56	N	
61	FTE 645	Sunbeam W	EE 406/8M 80hp	50083	Park Royal	H30/26R	10/44	12/65	U	Note D
62	FTE 646	Sunbeam W	EE 406/8M 80hp	50084	Park Royal	H30/26R	10/44	12/65	U	Note D
63	FTE 647	Sunbeam W	EE 406/8M 80hp	50089	Park Royal	H30/26R	11/44	4/63	U	Note E
64	FTE 648	Sunbeam W	EE 406/8M 80hp	50090	Park Royal	H30/26R	11/44	4/63	U	Note E
65	FTJ 401	Sunbeam W	MV207A3 85hp	50324	Roe	H30/26R	2/46	8/60	F	
66	FTJ 400	Sunbeam W	MV207A3 85hp	50325	Roe	H30/26R	3/46	8/60	F	
77	LTC 771	Crossley TDD42	MV209AYG1 95hp	94439	Crossley	H30/28R	1/50	8/63	U	Note F
78	LTC 772	Crossley TDD42	MV209AYG1 95hp	94440	Crossley	H30/26R	1/50	8/63	U	Note F
79	LTC 773	Crossley TDD42	MV209AYG1 95hp	94441	Crossley	H30/26R	2/50	8/63	U	Note F
80	LTC 774	Crossley TDD42	MV209AYG1 95hp	94442	Crossley	H30/26R	7/50	10/64	P	Note F, G
81	LTC 775	Crossley TDD42	MV209AYG1 95hp	94443	Crossley	H30/26R	7/50	8/63	U	Note F
82	YTE 821	BUT 9612T	MV209AWG1 95hp	9612T247	Bond	H33/28R	10/56	12/66	L	
83	YTE 822	BUT 9612T	MV209AWG1 95hp	9612T248	Bond	H33/28R	10/56	12/66	L	
84	YTE 823	BUT 9612T	MV209AWG1 95hp	9612T249	Bond	H33/28R	10/56	12/66	L	
85	YTE 824	BUT 9612T	MV209AWG1 95hp	9612T250	Bond	H33/28R	9/56	6/66	U	
86	YTE 825	BUT 9612T	MV209AWG1 95hp	9612T251	Bond	H33/28R	10/56	12/66	L	
87	YTE 826	BUT 9612T	MV209AWG1 95hp	9612T252	Bond	H33/28R	9/56	12/66	P	
88	YTE 827	BUT 9612T	MV209AWG1 95hp	9612T253	Bond	H33/28R	10/56	6/66	U	
89	YTE 828	BUT 9612T	MV209AWG1 95hp	9612T254	Bond	H33/28R	10/56	10/66	U	

Note A Appear to have been ordered as TB4 but built as TB6, which had the 6-inch longer wheelbase of the TB5. Fitted with trolley wheels enabling their use on Hathershaw route until that was abandoned in 1939.

Note B New 1936, Crossley prototype, finished in Crossley green and white livery, running mainly in Ashton. Purchased by Ashton 12/37. Fitted with trolley wheels for use on Hathershaw route until that was abandoned in 1939.

Note C New 1936 as Crossley prototype and demonstration vehicle, on trade plates, in Ashton livery and running mainly on Ashton's Hathershaw route. Purchased by Ashton 6/38. Fitted with trolley wheels for use on Hathershaw route until that was abandoned in 1939.

Note D Traction voltage lighting and no batteries until rebodied by Roe H33/28R, re-entering service 1/58.

Note E Traction voltage lighting and no batteries until rebodied by Bond H33/28R, re-entering service 12/55 and 12/54 respectively.

Note F Delivered 12/49 (77), 1/50 (78/9), 2/50 (81) and 3/50 (80).

Note G Withdrawn 8/63 with rest of batch and then reinstated due to requirement for an extra vehicle.

Note H Railless 54/55 were delivered with fleet numbers 55, 54. Those withdrawn in 1939 had been fitted with pneumatic tyres and rebuilt to B34R.

Ashton 66, a Sunbeam W with Roe utility body in the garage forecourt.
Sunbeam via Ian Allan Library

Service Vehicles

The most noticeable adjuncts to the trolleybuses were the 'tower wagons' which attended to the overhead wiring. A list of those which supported the trolleybuses is below, noting that they also serviced the tramway overhead. The first were built upon old AEC and Daimler motor-bus chassis and some of these solid machines, dating from the 1920s, lasted until after the war. Between 1937 and 1947 four forward-control Thornycrofts were purchased, and in 1945 a Leyland Tiger single-decker was converted to a tower wagon. Finally two new Guy Vixen tower wagons were obtained in 1957; these were ordered as Guy Otters with Gardner engines but Guy was building a large batch of Perkins-engined Vixens and the Department was persuaded (by offer of a substantial discount) to change. Both later passed to tramway duties with Blackpool Corporation. Towards the end of operation overhead work was carried out by the surviving Guy A120 and the youngest Thornycroft A118, which acted as spare. The latter was purchased in 1967 for preservation and is now in the Greater Manchester Museum of Transport.

It is beyond this book to list the breakdown cranes, lorries, vans, etc which were also used — all were also employed servicing the tram and motorbus fleets. Ford vans of all types, from the small 8hp to powerful V8, were used by the engineering staff to attend to vehicle failures. From 1955 onwards the Fords were replaced by BMC diesel 30cwt vans and the familiar all-red livery gave way to one of dark green.

Major breakdowns were attended by one of the two heavy cranes — a Bristol A-type and a Leyland Leviathan, both of which had been double-deck buses. An ex-government AEC Matador, rebuilt by the Department, took over these duties in the mid-fifties and other towing work was carried out by Fordson Major agricultural tractors and then an adapted Ford Thames Trader lorry. The Fordson tractors were fitted with a large buffer at the front by means of which they could push vehicles without damage. When the large roundabout was being built at Ardwick Green in the late 1950s, and the overhead was disconnected, trolleybuses had to negotiate the junction on their batteries and a tractor was stationed there to assist any with weak batteries.

The only vehicles used exclusively for overhead work, apart from the tower wagons, were a low loading reel wagon for carrying the wires and a pole-carrying trailer. These were towed by one of the Department's lorries. The Corporation Transport also owned a Jones Super 22 mobile crane which was used for the erection of poles.

Fleet No	Registration No	Chassis make & type	Date new or converted	Date withdrawn	Converted from
A111	NB 2167	AEC YC	-/19	7/43	bus NB 2167
none	NB 3546	Daimler Y	-/20	-/39	
A112	NB 2355	AEC YC	1/28	6/50	bus 7
A113	NF 1802	Daimler 36CM	5/33	2/52	bus 57
A114	DND 920	Thornycroft Dandy DF	4/37	11/57	
A115	DXJ 97	Thornycroft Dandy DF	11/37	10/57	
A116	DXJ 98	Thornycroft Dandy DF	11/37	11/57	
A117	VR 9675	Leyland Tiger TS2	3/45	4/58	bus 109
A118	HVM 93	Thornycroft Sturdy II	4/47	1/67	
A119	TVM 891	Guy Vixen LVDF	11/56	10/65	
A120	TVM 892	Guy Vixen LVDF	11/56	4/67	

Ashton Corporation had a Vulcan tower wagon until 1932 when 1923 Guy BA single-deck bus 41 (TC 4364) was converted. This lasted until a Bedford normal-control tower wagon (ETE 159) was purchased in 1939. Another Manchester veteran, 1921 Daimler Y NB 4728, which had always been a tower wagon, was sold to Ashton-under-Lyne in 1937 to provide an extra vehicle during the erection of trolleybus overhead. The SHMD Board favoured the Thornycroft and ran a 'Sturdy' tower wagon of this make (MMA 404), new 1950; its predecessor was also of this make, having been converted from Thornycroft LC single-deck bus 118 (LG 3043).

In April 1965, 1352 passes Ashton's Bedford tower wagon, ETE 159, at work completing the overhead at the new roundabout at Chester Square. It was the last new wiring on the system.
Peter Thompson

210 PICCADILLY — HYDE ROAD — DENTON — HYDE — GEE CROSS (8.90 miles)

Planned to commence	1939	as service 24; postponed due to war and then due to shortage of new trolleybuses
Renumbered	1948	planned to become 36
Motor bus conversion	15.3.48	tram 19 to motor bus 106
Trolleybus conversion	16.1.50	numbered 210 from motor bus 106 (Piccadilly — Hyde) and extended to Gee Cross
Terminus moved	17.12.56	from George Street to Portland Street, outside the then Queens Hotel
Partially converted	19.1.63	to bus 210 from 20.1.63
Last trolleybus	28.4.63	210 motor bus from 29.4.63

211 STEVENSON SQUARE — OLDHAM ROAD — BEN BRIERLEY — MOSTON, GARDENER'S ARMS — GREENGATE (4.84 miles)

Commenced	27.6.41	numbered 80x, Stevenson Square — Ben Brierley, replacing some journeys on bus 80 (Chorlton — Charlestown Road)
Extended and renumbered	14.7.41	bus 80 split, northern section replaced by trolleybus 37 from Stevenson Square — Nuthurst Road; peak hour shuttle bus to Charlestown Road numbered 80x
Extended and renumbered	2.8.41	36, extended to Gardener's Arms, 36x to Nuthurst Road, 37 to Ben Brierley
Extended	23.8.43	36 at peak hours to A. V. Roe works, Greengate, turning in private bus station
Renumbered	12.7.48	36 to 31, 37 to 31x. 36x not designated separately and rarely worked
Terminus moved	11.10.48	to new central island on Newton Street side of the square
Renumbered	31.8.53	31 to 211, 31x to 211x
Last trolleybus	7.8.55	reverted to cross-city motor bus 80 (Gardener's Arms — Chorlton, Hardy Lane) 8.8.55

212 CHURCH STREET — ROCHDALE ROAD — BEN BRIERLEY — MOSTON, GARDENER'S ARMS — GREENGATE (4.62 miles)

Commenced	4.11.40	trolleybus short workings on bus 55 (Ben Brierley or Nuthurst Road) to Moston Lane numbered 55x (out via Conran Street) or 60x (out via Rochdale Road); temporary terminus in Stevenson Square
Extended and renumbered	-.1 .41	to Ben Brierley, all journeys on 55 trolleybus operated, renumbered 32; 60x continues.
Extended	14.7.41	city terminus to Church Street (until around 1952 buses showed 'High Street' on the destination indicator); extended from Ben Brierley to Nuthurst Road, peak hour shuttle bus to Gardener's Arms
Extended and renumbered	2.8.41	32 to Gardener's Arms; 32x Nuthurst Road, 33 Ben Brierley, 33x Moston Lane out via Conran Street (pm rush hours), 34 Moston Lane out via Rochdale Road (am rush hour), use of 34 was rare until 1948 and the number did not appear in the timetable until 1952
Extended	23.8.43	32 at peak hours to A V Roe works, Greengate, turning in private bus station
Introduced	8.46	all-night trolleybus, 32x Church Street to Gardener's Arms
Revised	.47/48	all-night trolleybus terminus to Piccadilly, in via Newton Street, out via Stevenson Square
Renumbered	31.8.53	32 to 212, 33 to 212x, 33x, 34 to 214 (Nuthurst Road journeys ceased *circa* 1948)
Last trolleybus	23.4.55	on 214, motor bus 114x 25.4.55
Last trolleybus	24.4.55	on 212, 212x. Motor bus 112/113 (cross-city, Moston — Sale Moor) 25.4.55

212 AYTOUN STREET — AUDENSHAW (4.85 miles)

Commenced	17.6.57	due to new one-way system in Piccadilly. To avoid congestion in Portland Street, siding installed in Aytoun Street for loading outward peak hour short workings on 219. These were renumbered 212 (Audenshaw), 212x (Fairfield Road or Grey Mare Lane). For the same reason, some inward 212, 212x journeys terminated at London Road, using the Fairfield Street/Whitworth Street loop
Extended	by 3.59	212 to Snipe, other journeys then usually showed 212x and Guide Bridge journeys were 219x
Terminus moved	25.5.59	from Snipe to Ryecroft Hall as a result of new road system and roundabout
Converted	30.4.66	most journeys worked by motor bus
Last trolleybus	2.11.66	4.11.66 to motor bus 212

213 CORPORATION STREET (MILLER STREET) — ARDWICK GREEN — UNIVERSITY — GREENHEYS (4.16 miles)

Commenced	5/6.4.40	30 Rochdale Road (Thompson Street) — University (Brunswick Street, New York Street), conversion of 51 tram
Extended	21.1.46	to Moss Lane East (delayed from 14.1.46)
Extended	20.2.46	to Platt Lane
Extended	12.7.48	to Corporation Street, turning via Mayes Street and Redfern Street
Renumbered	21.4.52	213
Last trolleybus	31.5.59	1.6.59 to motor bus 123

214 CHURCH STREET — MOSTON LANE *see 212*

215 STEVENSON SQUARE — ASHTON NEW ROAD — AUDENSHAW, SNIPE (4.86 miles)

Commenced	31.7.38	numbered 27, former tram 26B. All-day short workings 27x Stevenson Square — Edge Lane
Introduced	14.7.41	all-night service 27x Stevenson Square — Ashton New Road — Snipe — Ashton Old Road — Stevenson Square
Revised	8.46	all-night revised 27x Stevenson Square — Snipe in and out via Ashton New Road, 28x all-night on Ashton Old Road
Revised	.47/48	all-night terminus to Piccadilly, in via Newton Street, out via Stevenson Square
Renumbered	17.4.50	27 to 215, 27x to 215x
Terminus moved	17.6.57	215x all-night service terminus moved to Stevenson Square from Piccadilly due to one-way system
Revised	27.1.58	half of 215x all-day off-peak journeys to Edge Lane replaced by motor bus 46 to Sunnyside Road, joint with Mayne
Terminus moved	25.5.59	from Snipe to Ryecroft Hall as a result of new road system and roundabout
Revised	19.7.64	all-night trolleybus journeys to motor bus
Revised	20.7.64	motor bus all-day Sunday
Revised	27.8.66	motor bus all-day Saturdays
Last trolleybus	30.12.66	31.12.66 to motor bus 215, 215x

216 STEVENSON SQUARE — ASHTON NEW ROAD — ASHTON-UNDER-LYNE — STALYBRIDGE (7.89 miles)

Commenced	31.7.38	numbered 26 — former 26 tram service, which had been cut back to the Snipe as 26B when trolleybus 28 started, the Snipe — Stalybridge section being temporarily covered by journeys on trolleybus 28 and Ashton motor bus service 1
Extended	27.2.39	to Stalybridge, replacing Ashton motor bus service 1
Renumbered	17.4.50	26 to 216
Revised	8.8.55	216X peak hour terminus moved to Newton Street (opposite GPO) due to congestion in Stevenson Square
Revised	18.2.57	216X terminus moved back to Stevenson Square
Terminus moved	26.11.59	into new Stalybridge Bus Station, in via Market Street, out via Waterloo Road
Last trolleybus	30.12.66	31.12.66 motor bus 216, 216x

217 ASHTON-UNDER-LYNE — GUIDE BRIDGE — DENTON — HAUGHTON GREEN (4.41 miles)

Commenced	1.7.40	Converted from bus 57, wiring completed only to Denton, shuttle bus thence to Haughton Green
Extended	9.12.40	to Haughton Green
Renumbered	7.47	17 (Ashton series service number)
Renumbered	17.4.50	from 17 to 217
Last trolleybus	3.7.60	4.7.60 to motor bus 127

218 PICCADILLY — ASHTON OLD ROAD — ASHTON-UNDER-LYNE — STALYBRIDGE (7.88 miles)

Commenced	1.3.38	28 (Piccadilly — Stalybridge), converted from tram 28 and extended from Ashton to Stalybridge
Introduced	21.3.38	all-day short workings 29 (Piccadilly — Audenshaw Road (Trough), 29x (Piccadilly — Fairfield Road)
Introduced	31.7.38	29 extended to Snipe and renumbered 28x (Piccadilly — Snipe); 29 (Trough) then rush hours only, all-day 29x (Fairfield Road) continues
Renumbered	16.10.39	29 to 31, 29x to 31x to allow Guide Bridge service to become 29
Renumbered	by 4.43	31 renumbered 29x (to avoid clash with MCT operation of bus 31 to Bramhall), 31x continues
Introduced	8.46	all-night 28x Piccadilly — Snipe in and out via Ashton New Road
Renumbered	12.7.48	31x also to 29x — see 219
Renumbered	17.4.50	28 to 218, 28x to 218x
Revised	4.51	some all-night journeys to Guide Bridge numbered 219x; always shown as 218x in timetable
Terminus moved	16.6.57	across Portland Street to outside the then Queens Hotel, in connection with Piccadilly one-way system
Terminus moved	25.5.59	218x from Snipe to Ryecroft Hall as a result of new road system and roundabout
Terminus moved	26.11.59	into new Stalybridge Bus Station, in via Market Street, out via Waterloo Road
Converted	19.7.64	all-night 218x to motor bus
Partially converted	20.7.64	motor buses work some journeys, Manchester use motor buses on Saturdays
Partially converted	1.5.66	last regular Manchester 218 trolleybus; Ashton continues to work trolleybuses on 218
Last trolleybus	30.12.66	31.12.66 to motor bus 218

219 PICCADILLY — ASHTON OLD ROAD — GUIDE BRIDGE — ASHTON-UNDER-LYNE (6.88 miles)

Commenced	16.10.39	29 Piccadilly — Guide Bridge, converted from bus 15x (Piccadilly — Guide Bridge), bus 15 (Guide Bridge — Piccadilly -Worsley) continues to operate. All-day trolleybus journeys to Fairfield Road reduced to rush hour only; Trough and Fairfield Road journeys renumbered 31, 31x.
Extended	22.3.40	to Ashton; short working to Guide Bridge numbered 29x
Revised	10.3.41	to save fuel, bus 15 (Guide Bridge — Piccadilly — Worsley) divided in city, Guide Bridge section served by extra journeys on 29
Renumbered	17.4.50	29, 29x to 219, 219x
Revised	4.55	some all-night journeys altered to run to Guide Bridge, numbered 219x
Terminus moved	16.6.57	across Portland Street to outside the then Queens Hotel, in connection with Piccadilly one-way system
Renumbered	17.6.57	some journeys renumbered 212, 212x — see 212 (Aytoun Street)
Renumbered	by 3.59	212 journeys from Aytoun Street to Guide Bridge renumbered 219x
Converted	19.7.64	all-night 219x to motor bus
Revised	20.7.64	worked by motor bus all-day Sundays
Last trolleybus	10.10.64	11.10.64 to motor bus 219

1306 and 1333 in Stalybridge, the latter on driver training duties which would include practice in rewiring trolley booms. *Tony Belton*

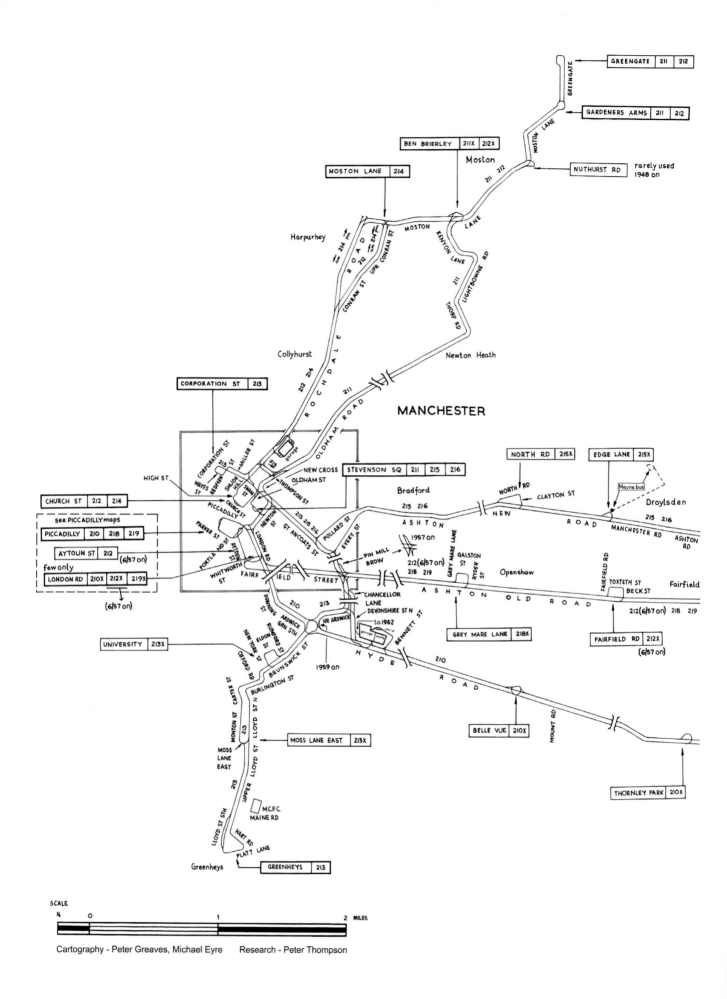

GREENGATE | 211 | 212

GARDENERS ARMS | 211 | 212

BEN BRIERLEY | 211X | 212X

Moston

MOSTON LANE | 214

NUTHURST RD   rarely used 1948 on

MOSTON LANE

GREENGATE

211 212

211

Harpurhey

on 214 PM
on 214 PM
212
213

KENYON LANE

LIGHTBOWNE RD

211

THORP RD

Newton Heath

Collyhurst

CONRAM ST
UPR CONRAM ST

MOSTON LANE

ROCHDALE ROAD

OLDHAM ROAD

212 214
211

CORPORATION ST | 213

MANCHESTER

NORTH RD | 215X

EDGE LANE | 215X

CORPORATION ST

MILLER ST

garage

NORTH RD

CLAYTON ST

Mayne bus

Droylsden

NEW CROSS

STEVENSON SQ | 211 | 215 | 216

ROAD

MANCHESTER RD

ASHTON RD

HIGH ST

MAYES ST
REDFERN ST
SMEDE HILL ST
SWAN ST

OLDHAM ST

Bradford

215 216

NEW

215 216

CHURCH ST | 212 | 214

THOMPSON ST

CHURCH ST

PICCADILLY

NEWTON ST

GT ANCOATS ST

POLLARD ST

ASHTON

see PICCADILLY maps

PICCADILLY | 210 | 218 | 219

PARKER ST

LONDON RD

213 215 216

EVERY ST

1957 on

GREY MARE LANE

GALSTON ST
RYDER ST

Openshaw

FAIRFIELD RD

AYTOUN ST | 212   (6/57 on)

few only

PORTLAND ST
AYTOUN ST
WHITWORTH ST

PIN MILL BROW

212(6/57 on)
218 219

TOXTETH ST
BECK ST

Fairfield

LONDON RD | 210X | 212X | 219X

FAIRFIELD ST

STREET

ASHTON OLD ROAD

212(6/57 on) 218 219

(6/57 on)

CHANCELLOR LANE
DEVONSHIRE ST N

GREY MARE LANE | 218X

FAIRFIELD RD | 212X

UNIVERSITY | 213X

210

213

HR ARDWICK

to 1962

(6/57 on)

DOWNING ST
ARDWICK GRN STH

garage

BENNETT ST

NEW YORK ST
ELDON ST
RUMFORD ST

1959 on

HYDE

ROAD

210

OXFORD RD

BRUNSWICK ST

BURLINGTON ST

BELLE VUE | 210X

MOSTON ST
CARTER ST

213

LLOYD ST N

MOSS LANE EAST | 213X

MOUNT RD

MOSS LANE EAST

UPPER LLOYD ST

M.C.F.C.
MAINE RD

THORNLEY PARK | 210X

LLOYD ST STH

213

HART RD

PLATT LANE

Greenheys

GREENHEYS | 213

SCALE

¼   0   1   2 MILES

Cartography - Peter Greaves, Michael Eyre   Research - Peter Thompson

Route Map

This map shows the maximum extent of each daytime route and its wiring, using the 210-219 service numbers.
The outer termini of 'X' short workings are shown; the inner terminus was that of the main service, apart from those Ashton Old Road and Hyde Road peak hour journeys which started or finished at London Road.
The map should be used in conjunction with the service lists, as the wiring shown did not all exist simultaneously; in particular, the 212, 212x Church Street - Moston service ended in 1955 and the 212, 212x service from Aytoun Street and London Road along Ashton Old Road commenced in 1957.

For readability, some of the junctions are shown at greater extent than they were 'on the ground'. Major wiring alterations are noted; there were many more minor changes.

The routes and wiring in the Piccadilly area were subject to major revision and are shown on a separate map.

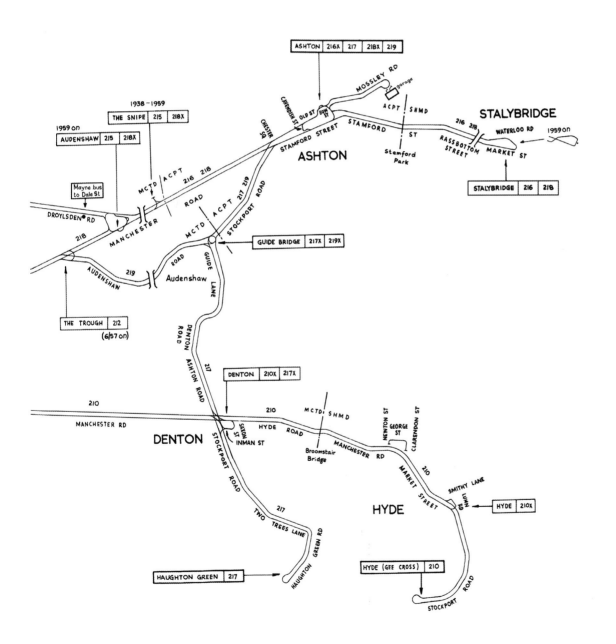

Piccadilly Area

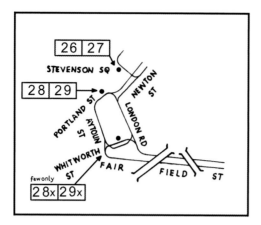

1938

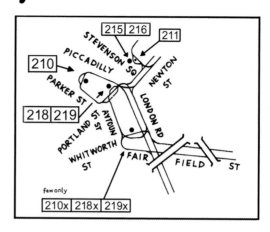

Jan 1950 to Dec 1956
showing 21-series service numbers

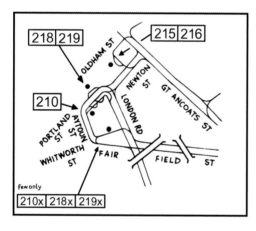

Dec 1956 to June 1957

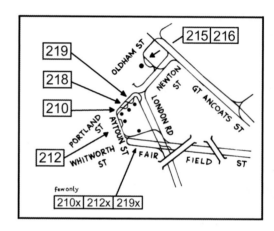

June 1957 onwards

The sidings in Portland Street and Aytoun Street were removed and other links simplified or taken out after each service was changed to motor bus

A complex three-track piece of overhead allowed a trolleybus to pass those waiting at any of the other Portland Street stops, which were neatly arranged in order — 210, then 218, then 219. Ashton 79 on the 218, with a similar Manchester and another Ashton Crossley behind on the 219.
Ted Jones

Destinations

Column 1 (destination blind):
STALYBRIDGE
ASHTON-UNDER-LYNE
AUDENSHAW THE SNIPE
AUDENSHAW RD THE TROUGH
FAIRFIELD RD
BESSEMER ST
GREY MARE LANE
LONDON RD
PICCADILLY
EDGE LANE
NORTH RD
POLLARD ST
STEVENSON SQ
ROCHDALE RD GARAGE
HYDE RD GARAGE
ROCHDALE RD
OXFORD RD UNIVERSITY
GREENHEYS MOSS LANE EAST
GREENHEYS PLATT LANE
HAUGHTON GREEN
DENTON
GUIDE BRIDGE
ASHTON VIA GUIDE BRIDGE
PICCADILLY VIA GUIDE BRIDGE
GREENGATE
GARDENERS ARMS
BLACKLEY ESTATE
NUTHURST RD
BEN BRIERLEY
MOSTON LANE
HIGH ST
CITY GRD
SPECIAL

ROCHDALE RD
UNIVERSITY
AYTOUN ST
PICCADILLY
ARDWICK GREEN
BELLE VUE
THORNLEY PARK
DENTON
HYDE GEE CROSS
HYDE
FOOTBALL MATCH
SPECIAL

Column 2 (destination blind):
LONDON RD STN
OPENSHAW
FAIRFIELD
GUIDE BRIDGE

CLAYTON
DROYLSDEN
AUDENSHAW
ASHTON

ASHTON NEW RD
BRADFORD
CLAYTON

GUIDE BRIDGE
DENTON

LONDON RD STN.
ASHTON OLD RD
OPENSHAW
FAIRFIELD
AUDENSHAW

GT ANCOATS ST
ARDWICK GREEN
BRUNSWICK ST

CLAYTON
DROYLSDEN
AUDENSHAW

COLLYHURST
QUEEN'S PARK

QUEEN'S PARK
BLACKLEY

MILES PLATTING
LIGHTBOWNE RD
MOSTON CEMETERY

ALL NIGHT
SERVICE

POST
BUS

Sections from Manchester trolleybus destination and intermediate blinds. They include the destination and intermediate displays that would have been used for the Blackley service.

The intermediate display "Post Bus" is worth a word of explanation. Up to 1941, the trams, bus and trolleybuses on certain evening journeys would carry a red Royal Mail letter box, clipped and locked to the rear of the bus. Anyone wishing to post a letter could go to a convenient bus stop, hail the bus, which would be displaying "POST BUS" on its indicators, and put the letter in the box. At the city terminus the boxes were collected by the Royal Mail and taken to the sorting office in Newton Street. There was no extra charge for this most useful service. It had to be given up due to fears of sabotage and was never reintroduced. This is the 1938 timetable, the facility being provided on trolleybus 26.
Chris Heaps, Michael Eyre

LETTER BOXES ON TRAMCARS and BUSES—Times of Departures

MONDAY TO FRIDAY ONLY.

Route No. 1. Bus pm
Gatley 8 50
Cheadle 8 53
Parrs Wood 8 58
Didsbury 9 1

Route No. 62. Bus
Heaton Park 9 11
Cheetham Hill 9 14
Albert Square 9 29

Route No. 81 Bus
Chorlton-cum-Hardy 9 9
Whalley Range (Seymour Gr.) 9 13
Brooks's Bar 9 17
Albert Square............ 9 30

Route No. 15X
Guide Bridge 8 52
Fairfield 8 59
Bessemer Street.......... 9 3
Chancery Lane 9 11
Piccadilly 9 20

Nos. 54 & 61 Bus pm   pm
Middleton Junc. — 8 43 —
Middleton 8 55 8 53 9 15
Blackley .... 9 3 — 9 23
Moston Lane .. 9 6 — 9 26
Collyhurst St... 9 11 — 9 33
Stevenson Sq... 9 20 — 9 40

Route No. 16. Bus
Heywood.................. 8 47
Hopwood 8 52
Middleton 9 5
Blackley 9 13
Harpurhey (Moston Lane) .. 9 17
Collyhurst Street 9 20
Cannon Street 9 30

Route No. 19
Hyde 8 35
Denton (Crown Point)..... 8 44
Gorton (Wellington St.) .. 8 56
West Gorton (Clowes St.).. 9 4
Ardwick 9 8
Piccadilly 9 20

Routes Nos. 20 & 21
Waterhead .... 8 35 —
Mumps............. 8 44 —
Oldham (Market Pl.) 8 49 —
Werneth........... 8 54 —
Hollinwood........ 9 5 8 58
Failsworth (Old Road) 9 10 9 3
Newton Heath 9 14 9 7
Miles Platting 9 21 9 15
Stevenson Square .... 9 31 —
Piccadilly .... — 9 27

Route No. 80. Bus pm
Chorlton-cum-Hardy 9 13
Alexandra Park 9 13
Junction 9 18
Piccadilly 9 28

Route No. 45 Bus
Benchill 8 45
Barlow Moor Road 9 1
Parker Street 9 22

Route No. 80 Bus
Moston 9 13
Piccadilly 9 31

Route No. 26. Trolley Bus
Stalybridge 8 40
Ashton 8 48
Audenshaw 8 55
Droylsden (Market St.) .. 9 0
Clayton (Edge Lane) 9 3
Bradford (Mill Street) .. 9 7
Beswick (Every Street)... 9 13
Stevenson Square 9 20

Route No. 32
Reddish 9 10
West Gorton (Library) ... 9 22
Ardwick 9 30
Corner of High Street and
  Market Street.......... 9 40

Routes Nos. 35 & 37
Hazel Grove .... 8 40 —
Stockport (Mersey Sq.) 8 59 —
Heaton Norris Station 9 2 —
Heaton Chapel ...... 9 6 —
Levenshulme (Lloyd R.) 9 9 9 17
Longsight(Dick'ns'n R.) 9 17 9 25
Ardwick 9 25 9 34
Piccadilly 9 33 9 42

Route No. 38B.
Mauldeth Road 9 8
West Point 9 13
Longsight (Dickenson Rd.) .. 9 18
Plymouth Grove (Upper
  Brook Street).......... 9 26
Albert Square........... 9 36

Route No. 40
East Didsbury (Parrs
  Wood)........... 8 46 9 0
Mauldeth Road 8 53 9 7
Moseley Road 8 56 9 10
Victoria Park (High S.) 9 3 9 17
Albert Square....... 9 17 9 31

Route No. 36
Barlow Moor Road 8 57
Moss Side 9 7
Albert Square............ 9 22

Route No. 64. Bus pm
Moss Nook 8 45
Gatley 8 54
Northenden 9 0
Parker Street 9 26

Route No. 76 Bus
Wilbraham Road 9 13
Claremont Road 9 18
Piccadilly............... 9 31

Routes Nos. 41 & 42
Chorlton-cum-Hardy
  (Hardy Lane) ...... — 9 0
West Didsbury 9 8 9 10
Withington(Burton R.) 9 10 9 12
Fallowfield 9 12 9 14
Rusholme 9 17 9 19
Piccadilly (Mosley St.) 9 33 9 35

Route No. 48. Bus
Altrincham .... 8 51 —
Timperley (W. Tim.S) 8 56 —
Marsland Road 9 2 8 56
Sale (School Road) .. 9 6 9 0
Stretford (Barton Rd) 9 11 9 4
Old Trafford Bar .. 9 21 9 14
St. Mary's Gate ... 9 33 9 25

Routes Nos. 49 & 49X Bus
Sale Moor .... 8 48 —
Sale Station........ 8 51 8 58
Stretford (Barton Rd.) 8 57 9 4
Old Trafford 9 3 9 14
Stretford R. (All Snts) 9 16 9 23
Piccadilly 9 24 9 34

Route No. 57
Audenshaw. 8 50
Denton 9 0
Transferred to Hyde car at Denton.

Route No. 59 & 77. Bus
Mills Hill Bridge 8 29
Middleton A 8 43
Rhodes 8 50
Middleton Road 8 53
Crumpsall 8 57
Great Clowes Street...... 9 4
Victoria Bridge 9 11
A—Transferred to 77 Bus at
  Middleton.

Route No. 54. Bus
Middleton Junc. 8 52
Lightbowne 8 57
Dean Lane 9 1
Queen's Road 9 8
Stevenson Square 9 18

Route No. 25. Bus
New Moston 8 55
Oldham Road 9 7
Culcheth Road 9 10
Bradford Road 9 18
Stevenson Square 9 28

Fourteen

The Supply Network

Manchester's electrical supply for its trolleybuses was fed from substations owned by the Corporation Electricity Department (later the North Western Electricity Board), most of it installed for the tramways. The numbers are the July 1953 rectifier capacity in kilowatts. The substation's name is in **bold**.

Ancoats, Great Ancoats Street	500	
Ashford Street, Ashton New Road, Beswick	500	
Bennett Street, Hyde Road, Ardwick	375	
Britannia Street, Pottery Lane, Ashton Old Road	500	
Clayton, Cantrell Street, Ashton New Road	500	
Denton East, Ashworth Street, Crown Point	500	
Dickinson Street Power Station, city centre	Rotary Converter	
Droylsden West, Charles Street, Edge Lane	375	
Gorton, Chapman Street, Hyde Road	500	
Hooley Hill, Guide Lane/Garden Street, Audenshaw	375	
Kershaw Lane, Manchester Road, Audenshaw	500	

Lightbowne, Tomlinson Street, Gardener's Arms	375	
Midland Street, Chancellor Lane, Ardwick	500	
Mill Lane, Two Trees Lane, Haughton Green	375	
Moss Side, Bowes Street, near bus garage	375	
Moston, Worsley Avenue, Ben Brierley	375	
Newton Heath, Hadfield Street, Thorp Road	500	
Oldham Road A, Radium Street, New Cross	Rotary Converter	
Openshaw, Cornwall Street, Ashton Old Road	500 and Rotary Converter	
Polygon, Brunswick Street, Ardwick Green	Rotary Converter	
Queens Road, Queens Park, Rochdale Road	500	
Rochdale Road Garage, built into the trolleybus garage	375	

From the substations power was fed through underground cables, some originally laid for the tramways, to feeder boxes situated in the pavement at the side of the road, about a mile apart. There were also "coupler" feeder boxes at section boundaries on the Ashton New and Old Roads and Great Ancoats Street which, provided voltage and conditions were correct, made an automatic connection between sections to allow load sharing. The boxes had a serial number which was painted on them; "missing" numbers were those serving the tram overhead.

Box No	Location	At	Fed from	Services (210-219 series)
1	Piccadilly	Queens Hotel/55 Piccadilly	Dickinson Street	210, 218, 219
2	Aytoun Street	Portland Street	Dickinson Street	210, 218, 219
3	Fairfield Street	Fire Station	Dickinson Street	210, 218, 219
12	Rochdale Road	Moore Street (garage forecourt)	Garage	212, 213
13	Rochdale Road	Queens Road	Queens Road	212
14	Rochdale Road	Conran Street	Queens Road	212
27	Oldham Road	Radium Street	Oldham Road A	211, 213
28	Oldham Road	Reather Street	Oldham Road A	211
29	Oldham Road	Monsall Road	Thorp Road	211
32	Thorp Road	Hadfield Street	Thorp Road	211
33	Moston Lane	Ben Brierley	Worsley Avenue	211, 212
34	Moston Lane	Worsefold Street	Worsley Avenue	211, 212
35	Moston Lane	Gardener's Arms, Greengate	Tomlinson Street	211, 212
39	Great Ancoats Street	Newton Street	Ancoats	213, 215, 216
40	Great Ancoats Street	Pollard Street	Ancoats	213, 215, 215
41	Pin Mill Brow	Palmerston Street	Midland Street	213, 215, 216
42	Pin Mill Brow	Ashton Old Road	Midland Street	213, 215, 216
43	Higher Ardwick	Union Street	Polygon	210, 213
44	Brunswick Street	Upper Brook Street	Polygon	213
45	Lloyd Street	Moss Lane East	Moss Side	213
46	Upper Lloyd Street	Claremont Road	Moss Side	213
48	Ashton New Road	Philips Park Road	Ashford Street	215, 216
49	Ashton New Road	Grey Mare Lane	Ashford Street	215, 216
50	Ashton New Road	Recreation Ground	Cantrell Street	215, 216
51	Ashton New Road	Bebbington Street	Cantrell Street	215, 216
52	Manchester Road	Edge Lane	Droylsden West	215, 216
53	Manchester Road	Scott Road	Droylsden West	215, 216
54	Droylsden Road	Kershaw Lane	Kershaw Lane	215, 216
55	Droylsden Road	Manchester Road	Kershaw Lane	215, 216, 218
56	Fairfield Street	Fire Station	Dickinson Street	218, 219
57	Ashton Old Road	Midland Street	Midland Street	213, 218, 219
58	Ashton Old Road	Gorton Road	Britannia Street	218, 219
59	Ashton Old Road	Britannia Street	Britannia Street	218, 219
60	Ashton Old Road	Cromwell Street	Openshaw	218, 219
61	Ashton Old Road	Tamworth Street	Openshaw	218, 219
62	Ashton Old Road	Edna Street	Openshaw	218, 219
63	Ashton Old Road	Fairfield Office	Openshaw	218, 219
64	Manchester Road	The Trough	Kershaw Lane	218, 219
65	Manchester Road	Kershaw Lane	Kershaw Lane	218, 219
66	Audenshaw Road	Kershaw Lane	Kershaw Lane	219
67	Guide Lane	Croft Street	Guide Bridge Station	217, 219
68	Denton Road	Stamford Road	Hooley Hill	217
69	Ashton Road	Frederick Street	Denton East	217
70	Ashton Road	Crown Point, Walker Street	Denton East	210, 217
71	Stockport Road	Market Place	Denton East	210, 217
72	Stockport Road	Tib Street	Mill Lane	217
73	Two Trees Lane	Mill Lane	Mill Lane	217

Records for the Hyde Road service have not survived; the boxes were noted as

Ardwick Green	*Coral Street*	*Polygon*	*210*
Hyde Road	*Bennett Street*	*Bennett Street*	*210*
Hyde Road	*Belle Vue Street*	*Bennett Street*	*210*
Hyde Road	*Chapman Street*	*Gorton*	*210*
Manchester Road	*Thornley Park*	*Gorton*	*210*
Manchester Road	*Windmill Lane*	*Denton East*	*210*
Hyde Road	*Moorside Lane*	*Denton East*	*210*

At the time of writing, two Manchester and two Ashton-under-Lyne trolleybuses are in museums open to the public.

Manchester BUT 1344 and Ashton BUT 87 are at the excellent East Anglia Transport Museum, Carlton Colville, Lowestoft. 1334 is in working condition and from time to time operates "under the wires" on the museum's trolleybus route, offering rides to visitors.

Crossleys Manchester 1250 and Ashton 80 are static exhibits in the Greater Manchester Museum of Transport in Cheetham Hill, about a mile from the Manchester city centre. The museum's collection also includes the former Manchester Thornycroft tower wagon A118.

Greater Manchester Museum of Transport
Boyle Street
Cheetham Hill
Manchester M8 8UW
0161 205 2122
www.gmts.co.uk

East Anglia Transport Museum
Chapel Road
Carlton Colville
Lowestoft NR33 8BL
01502 518459
www.eatm.org.uk

In September 1991 '90 years of Manchester Corporation trams and buses' was the subject of one of the Greater Manchester Museum of Transport's popular themed weekend events, with a gathering of many preserved Manchester vehicles in Heaton Park. Manchester 1250 was towed to the display in the park, where it was joined by Manchester 1344 before the latter was taken to East Anglia. Also on display was Thornycroft tower wagon A118, which is also part of the Museum's collection.
GMTS collection

Requiem for a trolleybus system

The Fairfield Road turn-back is abandoned and a band plays as it leads a Remembrance Day
procession past Guy tower wagon A120, its crew dismantling the Beck Street overhead.
November 1966. *Chris Heaps*